Venture Forth!

Venture Forth!

The Essential Guide to Starting a Moneymaking Business in Your Nonprofit Organization

by Rolfe Larson

FIELDSTONE
ALLIANCE

SAINT PAUL,
MINNESOTA

We thank The David and Lucile Packard Foundation
for support of this publication.

Fieldstone Alliance is committed to strengthening the performance of the nonprofit sector. Through the synergy of its consulting, training, publishing, and research and demonstration projects, Fieldstone Alliance provides solutions to issues facing the nonprofit sector. Fieldstone Alliance was formerly a department of the Amherst H. Wilder Foundation. If you would like more information about Fieldstone Alliance and our services, please contact Fieldstone Alliance, 60 Plato Boulevard East, Suite 150, Saint Paul, MN 55107, 651-556-4500

We hope you find this book useful! For information about other Fieldstone Alliance publications, please see the order form on the last page or contact:

Fieldstone Alliance Publishing Center
60 Plato Boulevard East
Suite 150
Saint Paul, MN 55107
800-274-6024
www.FieldstoneAlliance.org

Edited by Vincent Hyman
Designed by Kirsten Nielsen
Illustrated by Russ McMullin
Cover design by Rebecca Andrews

Manufactured in the United States of America

Second printing, August 2005

Library of Congress Cataloging-in-Publication Data
Larson, Rolfe, 1953-
   Venture forth! : the essential guide to starting a moneymaking business in your nonprofit organization / by Rolfe Larson.
      p. cm.
   Includes bibliographical references and index.
   ISBN 0-940069-24-5 (pbk.)
   1. New business enterprises. 2. Nonprofit organizations.
I. Title.
   HD62.5 .L368 2002
   658.1'148—dc21   2001006566

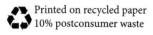

About the Author

ROLFE LARSON has twenty years of experience as a manager and consultant for nonprofit organizations. He is currently the president of Rolfe Larson Associates, a marketing, new venture, and Internet-commerce consulting firm located in Saint Paul, Minnesota, and online at www.RolfeLarson.com. This firm helps nonprofits and small businesses evaluate venture opportunities; develop new products, services, and distribution channels; and design effective marketing strategies. Examples of this work include market and feasibility studies, as well as marketing and business plans.

Rolfe is also an adjunct marketing professor at the University of St. Thomas in Minneapolis, Minnesota and a senior associate at The National Center for Social Entrepreneurs. His nonprofit management experience includes eight years as a senior manager at Minnesota Public Radio.

Rolfe earned a master's degree in business administration from Yale University's School of Management and a bachelor of arts degree from Swarthmore College. He has served on numerous nonprofit boards, including chairing the Nature Conservancy of Minnesota board of directors.

Acknowledgements

I am indebted to those who helped bring this book to fruition. Vince Hyman, Becky Andrews, and Kirsten Nielsen of Fieldstone Alliance demonstrated their passion for the printed word in a multitude of skilled ways. I could not imagine better guides through the mysteries and intricacies of the publishing world.

I wish to express gratitude to the nonprofit managers and consultants who reviewed and offered helpful advice on an initial draft of this book. Those reviewers were

Emil Angelica	J. Scott Craig	Judd Larson
Bryan Barry	Carol Gardner	Carol Lukas
Mary Birchard	Scott Gelzer	Carter McNamara
Jerr Boschee	John L. German	Jon McTaggart
Peter C. Brown	Beth Harper Briglia	Lisa Olszak
Kathleen E. Buescher	Mary C. Hoke	David Schachtner
Mike Burns	Andy Horsnell	Karen Simmons
Paul Connolly	Thomas J. Kigin	Jim Thalhuber
Mary Connolly-Ross	Charles L. Lacoste, Jr.	Paul Wasserman

Special thanks to William H. Kling, Jr., president of Minnesota Public Radio (MPR), who during my eight years working at MPR taught me by his example that entrepreneurs see opportunities where others see barriers; and to Thomas J. Kigin, MPR's executive vice president, whose quiet brilliance, financial acumen, and clarity of thought were an inspiration to me. I am also indebted to Frances Brody and John Weiser, of Brody•Weiser•Burns, who introduced me to the world of consulting with nonprofit organizations. Thanks also to Peter C. Brown, who has willingly offered invaluable advice and networking support at several key points in my career.

Appreciation should be extended to Jim Thalhuber and Mary Birchard, of The National Center for Social Entrepreneurs, for permission to include in this book adaptations of consulting materials they developed. Most notably among these are discussions about project leaders, core competencies, success factors, and entrepreneurial committees, and several worksheets in Chapters Two and Three. In addition, projects I worked on with The National Center for Social Entrepreneurs formed the basis for the case examples in Figure 2 and Worksheets 2B, 4A, and 4B.

Finally, I want to acknowledge the central role that my late father, Raeder Larson, and my mother, Sue Larson, played in teaching the importance of giving back to the community. Most important, this book would never have seen the light of day without the loving support, and sharp editing skills, of Annette Halley.

Rolfe Larson

March 2002

Contents

Introduction

Many nonprofits are adding another tool to their funding toolbox...

- The American Diabetes Association produces Gift of Hope, a holiday card and gift catalog. Proceeds of nearly $1 million per year support research to find a cure for diabetes.

- Families First, Inc., a social service agency in Atlanta, Georiga, created Trans-Parenting, a program that teaches effective techniques for parenting after a divorce. The local court system pays for the workshops on a fee-for-service basis. The nonprofit also sells the training and materials to more than 180 agencies nationwide.

- Project Turnabout, a residential compulsive gambling and substance abuse treatment facility in Granite Falls, Minnesota, bought a small motel to provide temporary off-campus housing for program clients. The agency earns income by renting out half of the rooms to the general public.

Each of these organizations is borrowing skills and techniques from the private sector. They are, in effect, running a business, attracting customers, and earning income like a private company, while pursuing both financial and mission-related goals. Also known as *nonprofit business development, earned income ventures, social entrepreneurship, social ventures,* or *social purpose businesses,* these activities help many nonprofits diversify funding, build stronger relationships with constituents, and improve visibility in the community.

What is a Venture?

A *venture* is any activity that involves selling products or services to customers. Three such ventures are listed above. Ventures developed by nonprofit organizations often have additional, mission-related objectives. However, the goal of earning income from sales to customers is what makes a venture different from other nonprofit activities.

Venture development is the process of finding and converting good venture ideas into a business. Building on the experience of many organizations, this workbook presents a time-tested approach for finding, testing, and launching a successful nonprofit venture.

For nonprofits, many business techniques transfer directly from the private sector, but others require tuning. This book offers a practical, step-by-step guide specifically for nonprofits, presenting what managers need to bring venture development into their organizations. It will help you decide how venture development fits into your organization, where to look for good venture ideas, how to determine if they are feasible, and how to write a strong business plan to start a successful venture.

> *"Most nonprofits have plenty of ideas on how to earn more money. What they need is help finding and following a structure, discipline, and process to move forward with their best ideas."*
>
> — *Jim Thalhuber, president, The National Center for Social Entrepreneurs* [1]

Why Pursue Ventures?

The most obvious reason to pursue ventures is to increase your funding base. Ventures generate dollars that help diversify your nonprofit's finances or pay expenses for which funding is difficult to come by.

There are several other good reasons to learn venture development skills. Nonprofits today operate in a dynamic world. Needs change, funders discover new interests, competitors emerge from unexpected places, and new service opportunities arise. Venture development can help you manage the inevitable changes by giving you skills to evaluate opportunities and risks from a business perspective.

Venture development techniques can also reduce your risks. An important part of the venture development process is gathering information—about your organization, your constituents, your allies and competitors, and the environment you operate in. Venture development provides a guide to gathering the right information and a framework for analyzing it. In this way, you can make decisions based on data rather than impressions.

Finally, the venture development process can help you allocate resources more effectively. By finding out what activities really cost—in money and staff time—you will be in a better position to decide where to direct your organization's energies.

Who Should Pursue Ventures?

This book is for nonprofit managers and board members who want a hands-on guide to business planning and venture development. Others who work with nonprofits—including consultants, lawyers, accountants, trainers, and funders—will also find this book useful. The steps presented here have been used with dozens of organizations, and experience has shown that they work for both large and small nonprofits, and for nonprofits that take a variety of legal forms. While this book presumes that an organization is currently contemplating a new venture, organizations already operating a venture will find these steps useful for evaluating, expanding, or improving their current offerings.

The steps presented here have been used with dozens of organizations, and experience has shown that they work for both large and small nonprofits.

How to Use This Book

This workbook is divided into four chapters that cover seven steps to developing a nonprofit business venture.

- *Chapter One: Venture Development Overview* explains what ventures are, what benefits and risks are involved, and what venture development looks like.

- *Chapter Two: Prospecting for Ventures* takes you through the first three steps of venture development. You'll get organized, which includes selecting a venture team and a project leader. You'll conduct a venture audit, which involves candidly assessing your organization's entrepreneurial capabilities and clarifying whom you serve and what you do best. Finally, you'll brainstorm venture possibilities and then screen those ideas to find the most promising ones.

- *Chapter Three: Testing the Feasibility of Your Venture Ideas* takes you through Steps 4, 5, and 6. You will put your best venture ideas through a quick market test to select the one most likely to succeed. You'll do the really heavy lifting of venture development—market research and financial analysis.

- *Chapter Four: Business Planning* ties together all the work of the previous steps. You'll write a compelling and detailed business plan, gain approval and financing for it, and get ready to embark on your new venture.

Each chapter contains worksheets, examples, and tips to guide you through the seven steps. To gain the most from this book, take the time to review and complete each worksheet. The worksheets break the work into manageable pieces. By working through them carefully, you won't miss anything important. The worksheets also tie together neatly to form the bulk of your business plan—all you need do is clean them up for your final audience. If you fill them out using a word processing program, you should be able to cut and paste them quickly into a business plan.

Appendix G contains blank copies of all the worksheets for you to copy and use for your own venture ideas. These worksheets are also available for downloading from the Wilder Publishing Center's web site. (Instructions for accessing the worksheets online are provided in Appendix G.) The appendices also include a bibliography and a list of helpful resources, such as venture-related Internet sites.

Before you do anything else, set aside a couple of hours and read through the book. Go ahead and skim, but read carefully enough to get the big picture. Be sure you are clear on the differences between a venture audit, a feasibility analysis, and a business plan. Then, when you're ready, sharpen a pencil or two, and dive into that first worksheet. Good luck!

Chapter One

Venture Development Overview

$\mathbf{T}$his chapter gives you a broad perspective on venture development. It identifies the benefits and limitations of doing ventures, and describes the differences in how nonprofit and for-profit companies approach this topic. Finally, it summarizes and gives a time estimate for each of the seven venture development steps.

By the end of the chapter you should have a better understanding of the issues surrounding venture development, and of the process presented in this book for developing your own ventures.

Nonprofit Ventures: An Oxymoron?

Since one purpose of a venture is to earn money, it may seem like a contradiction in terms for a *non*profit to go into business. However, nonprofit organizations are permitted to earn money, including profits; their nonprofit status simply precludes distribution of any surplus to those with a controlling interest in the organization, such as officers, directors, or staff.

Moreover, earning money is hardly a new concept for nonprofit organizations. Your organization already engages in venture activities if, for example, you charge fees for some services, you make publications available for sale, or you sublease space to another organization. In fact, depending on the category of nonprofit organization, the national averages for earned income as a percentage of budget ranges from 19 percent to 56 percent.[2]

Interest in nonprofit ventures has been growing. Government funding of nonprofits has been declining while the need for nonprofit services has been increasing each year. Many foundations would like to see nonprofits diversify their funding sources through venture development; a few have even helped fund these efforts.

Moreover, many nonprofits are experiencing competition from for-profit companies in areas that were previously the exclusive domain of the nonprofit sector. The Discovery Channel, for example, competes unabashedly with the Public Broadcasting Service.

Can nonprofits go into business?

In a word, yes. Most nonprofit organizations are free to engage in ventures as long as proceeds are used to support the organization's mission. Moreover, if these activities are *related* to the nonprofit's tax-exempt purpose—for example, a senior center selling a guide to senior health care services—ventures generally can be engaged in without limitation and without incurring income taxes.

Nonprofits can also engage in business activities that are deemed *unrelated* (for example, opening a coffee shop next door to the senior center). In these cases, the nonprofit must pay income taxes on profits derived from those activities. The Internal Revenue Service calls these taxes *unrelated business income taxes* (UBIT). Some nonprofits operate ventures that sell a mixture of related and unrelated products, paying UBIT on the unrelated portion. (Appendix E contains information from the IRS's web site on the unrelated business income tax issue.)

Unlike private sector firms, nonprofits face limitations on the amount of unrelated business activity they can engage in and still maintain their tax-exempt status. Unfortunately, no hard-and-fast rules govern this amount. An often quoted (but never officially documented) conservative guideline is that unrelated business activities are not a problem as long as they represent no more than 20 percent of the nonprofit's activity, measured, for example, by budget or staff.

If the unrelated business activity becomes too big, one option for the nonprofit organization is to establish a for-profit subsidiary, which allows the tax-paying venture to grow without threatening the nonprofit's tax-exempt status. But don't rush out to create a for-profit subsidiary unless it's necessary; in a variety of expected and unexpected ways it can be expensive to form and maintain a separate company.

Finally, in rare cases, some nonprofits are restricted from doing ventures of any kind because of their organizing documents or their contractual relationships with a major funder. Be sure to discuss these issues with qualified legal counsel.

Differences from private business

A nonprofit venture is fundamentally different from a for-profit business in that its earnings are not available to enrich those who control the organization. Also,

---

An often quoted (but never officially documented) guideline is that unrelated business activities are not a problem as long as they represent no more than 20 percent of the nonprofit's activity, measured, for example, by budget or staff.

nonprofits generally avoid offering products that conflict with their mission, even if doing so reduces income. No one is surprised if a hospital doesn't sell cigarettes in its coffee shop.

Another difference is that attitudes within nonprofits can hinder the ability to make money from venture activities. At issue often is whether earning income is appropriate in the first place. Some staff and supporters of nonprofits feel they should not be concerned with making money; in their thinking, making money is the role of the private sector. They believe that the nonprofit's mission transcends such concerns, or that the application of business principles will inevitably diminish, rather than expand, the organization's ability to serve. While there exist many examples of nonprofits that excel at both mission and profit, this concern still persists in some nonprofits.

> The information presented in this section should not be construed as legal advice. For more information, review Internal Revenue Service documents, such as Publication 598, *Tax on Unrelated Business Income of Exempt Organizations*, or visit the IRS web site at www.irs.gov. Be sure to consult with specialized legal counsel before making final tax and legal decisions.

A similar controversy concerns marketing and promotional efforts. Most nonprofits find that insufficient funding, not insufficient promotions, limits how much they can accomplish. For that reason, some staff may be uncomfortable with diverting scarce resources into promotional activities, in effect taking dollars away from achieving their mission. These staff members also might believe that competition is something to be avoided, that there is no need to pursue an idea if another organization in the community is doing something similar.

Venture activity turns each of these attitudes upside down. Profits earned to support the mission, marketing to improve relationships with constituencies, and competition that pushes the nonprofit to improve service and efficiency are all desirable elements of the venture mind-set. The point is, to fully benefit from the concepts described in this book, your nonprofit may need to work as much on attitudes as it does on activities. This kind of cultural change takes time, and a good way to start the process is to follow the steps in this book.

Similarities with private business

In most ways, managers of a nonprofit venture address the same issues faced by their counterparts in the for-profit sector. You must determine what customers want, find a cost-effective way to provide it, and persuade them that your product or service is the better choice among similar offerings. To stay in business, the venture's revenues must exceed costs. Competitors will try to win over your customers, and you will want to attract theirs. You and your competitors will also look for ways to become more efficient and to provide more of what customers want while eliminating things that they do not value.

Quick profits are a rarity in private business, and they are just as rare in the nonprofit sector. Starting and growing a venture is usually a long-term proposition. Ventures incur costs before they get their first customer, and most lose money—sometimes for years—while they pursue profitability.

No matter how much research and preparation you do, uncertainty lurks around every entrepreneurial corner. Thus, although a key purpose of ventures is to earn money, there is the risk of losing money. Following the steps in this book will increase your chance of success. Still, there are no guarantees.

Perhaps most important, the greatest similarity with private business is a single-minded focus on pursuing *opportunities* wherever they may lead. Often, with careful research, planning, intuition, and creativity, nonprofit managers can use ventures to inspire staff, serve constituencies in new ways, and provide the nonprofit with additional dollars.

Venture Benefits

A successful business venture can nourish a nonprofit in a variety of ways that enable it to extend its reach and effectiveness.

Improve finances

Ventures can help pay for expenses that are difficult to cover through fundraising, such as overhead and administrative expenses. Ventures can also subsidize programs for which funding is unavailable or too limited. Once money is earned from a venture, the nonprofit is generally free to spend it in any manner consistent with its mission and without the restrictions and reporting requirements that come with grants.

For most nonprofits it is unrealistic to expect that ventures could ever complete-ly replace traditional funding sources. Even the most successful ventures seldom provide more than one-third to one-half of an organization's annual budget. Thus, it

---

Thrift shop shifts focus from volunteers to customers

A women's center in Pennsylvania wanted to have a thrift shop, according to Karen Simmons, director of La Salle University Nonprofit Center—"just a little thrift shop that our volunteers could run, so we could earn a bit more money to support our domestic violence and hotline work. The shop became so popular that our dedicated volunteers couldn't keep up. For example, the public wanted our shop open nights and weekends, but the volunteers only wanted to work days. We had to shift our focus from the volunteers to the market, and it caused tremendous internal angst. Now that we've come through the changes, we're clear that this is a market-based activity and we have to keep our ear to the ground to meet market demands. The market is primary, and our volunteers are secondary. This was a huge shift for us, but one that needed to be made in order to be successful."[3]

is important to look at ventures as an opportunity to *expand* the earned-income portion of your budget and to *reduce* your dependence on grants and other traditional nonprofit funding sources. A common long-term goal for many nonprofits pursuing venture development is to increase earned income by an amount equal to ten or fifteen percentage points of their annual budget.

Even if they do not intend to earn unrelated income, many organizations improve their finances by using venture techniques to evaluate existing programs. For example, SENIORS FIRST, INC., an Orlando, Florida, nonprofit with an adult day care program used market research to discover that (1) it was not the preferred local provider of this program, (2) the adult day care cost more to run than the organization was receiving from fees and grants, and (3) its competitors had extra capacity. Based on its research, which was performed during a project with The National Center for Social Entrepreneurs, the nonprofit cancelled the adult day care program. Current customers were referred to competitors having extra capacity and equal or better quality. The nonprofit then used the substantial annual savings and the freed staff time to launch a new program to address an unmet community need.

Strengthen relationships with existing constituencies

Nonprofit organizations routinely seek additional ways to connect with members, funders, clients, volunteers, and other constituents to foster relationships and increase the nonprofit's impact. As described later in this book, one of the first places to look for customers is among your existing constituents. This broadening of relationships may bring them closer to your nonprofit and its purpose.

More and more nonprofits now offer food and beverages within their facilities as a way of strengthening relationships. A restaurant in a museum encourages visitors to stay longer and explore more exhibits. In some cases, such as a coffee shop located inside a public library, the venture also becomes a destination that attracts people to the nonprofit. A latte and that library book to go, please.

Increase visibility

Ventures can help nonprofits secure favorable press coverage and increase public awareness, thus raising the organization's name recognition. This enhanced visibility can be leveraged to attract volunteers, board members, fundraising dollars, and committed staff, and generally to help the nonprofit get its message out. For example, the Saint Paul Neighborhood Energy Consortium, a nonprofit environmental organization, manufactures a line of attractive garden products from used wood diverted from landfills. Sales of these products at gardening stores underscores the consortium's message that taking good care of the earth involves what you buy as well as what you place on the curb on recycling day.[4]

"We had to shift our focus from the volunteers to the market. Now that we've come through the changes, we're clear that this is a market-based activity and we have to keep our ear to the ground to meet market demands."

Combine financial and mission goals

Nonprofit ventures are often designed to pursue a combination of financial and mission-related goals. Some are formed with the explicit purpose of providing employment or job training to needy clients. For example, sheltered workshops hire individuals with physical or mental handicaps; venture managers are able to sell the services of these workshops partially on the basis of the social benefits they offer. Such socially beneficial, "affirmative" businesses serve an important social mission, and, while revenues rarely cover all their costs, the sales dollars they do generate help reduce dependence on grants.

Look at ventures as an opportunity to *expand* the earned-income portion of your budget and to *reduce* your dependence on grants.

Some ventures based on mission turn out to be good business decisions as well. For example, Dharma Publishing, located in Berkeley, California, was founded to promote Buddhist education and attitudes in the West. To help support this mission financially, several of its members launched a commercial printing shop. The members of the Buddhist organization who worked at the shop appreciated its unique atmosphere and philosophy that supported their religious practice. In turn, they were willing to work for moderate wages. The shop became known for the quality of its work furthered by the good attitude and willingness of its workers. Over the course of a ten-year period, the printing shop venture provided about $8 million of support to the nonprofit.[5]

Venture Limitations

Ventures are not for everybody, and they don't always work out as expected. Entrepreneurial efforts can lead to unpleasant surprises.

Profitability is not guaranteed

Some ventures flourish, others fail. A certain number of small businesses start with great promise, never become profitable, and then quietly shut down. Ventures started by nonprofit groups face similar uncertainties. While there are many examples of successful nonprofit venture development, there are also many cases where the effort failed, consuming resources that could have been used elsewhere.

Getting the right person to run the venture, performing the necessary research to complete a realistic business plan, and constantly improving the venture as your understanding of customers and competitors improves—issues that are addressed in this workbook—are key predictors of success in venture development. But they cannot guarantee success. The best-made plans of even the most skilled entrepreneurs can be dashed by the unpredictable swings of the marketplace.

Venture development may not suit your nonprofit

Some nonprofits are well suited for ventures, others are not. Ventures require flexibility in staffing, budgets, and decision making. It is better to discover early on that ventures are not appropriate for your organization or that the timing is not right. The sidebar "Do ventures fit with your nonprofit" on page 12 shows characteristics of nonprofits most likely to succeed with ventures. This topic is addressed in more detail in Chapter Two.

Ventures may clash with your culture or values

Nonprofits are typically formed to address an unmet need, advocate an important cause, educate constituents, or provide important social services. A venture, on the other hand, is charged with earning income from paying customers. When a nonprofit manager sets out to introduce attributes of the for-profit sector into the organization, internal friction often emerges. Some staff may believe that the organization's core values will disappear as the organization changes. It is often difficult and time-consuming to change the internal culture of a nonprofit to embrace ventures.

Similarly, nonprofit groups may also receive public criticism for pursuing ventures as an alternative source of revenue. Paradoxically, such criticism typically accompanies success. In today's shifting economy, nonprofits may find themselves in direct competition with a for-profit company, one that might not appreciate the rivalry. And, if the nonprofit is able to avoid paying income taxes on the venture, claims may surface about "unfair" competition.

> **Social Return on Investment (SROI)**
>
> Social return on investment, or SROI, is an emerging field of study that strives to quantify the social benefit that nonprofit endeavors create. SROI might enable a nonprofit to measure a venture's social return with the same currency, dollars, that it uses to calculate financial return. A nonprofit could use this metric to demonstrate the value of a venture to its board or to a potential philanthropic funder. Further details on SROI are available from the Roberts Enterprise Development Fund at www.redf.org.

Ventures may generate unfavorable publicity

In recent years, many YMCAs and YWCAs have constructed fitness facilities that rival those found in private health clubs. The competition has prompted complaints leading to congressional hearings and increased IRS review of nonprofit fitness centers. It is not unusual in such cases for articles criticizing the nonprofit to appear in local papers. While some organizations have policies against operating ventures that compete with for-profit companies, most recognize that in business you can't please everybody. Ventures are not for the weakhearted.

Start-up financing may be difficult to find

Most banks and other lending institutions are unfamiliar with nonprofit ventures, and tend to shy away from making loans for this purpose. In addition, they are understandably worried that if the nonprofit defaults on the loan, attempts to collect on the collateral would expose them to accusations that they are harming a valued community service.

Foundations and other philanthropists are also reluctant to provide start-up funding for nonprofit ventures. This is changing, slowly. The start-up cash crunch can make it difficult for a nonprofit to launch a venture.

On the other hand, it's a fact of business life that most start-up companies *are* strapped for cash when they first open their doors. Many successful small businesses turn this into an advantage, encouraging creativity and efficiency not often found when resources are plentiful.

Here's what one successful entrepreneur said:

> *"Start as small as possible: To achieve 100 percent success, you need to grow organically. Pass up outside financing until you know that you can run the company. Starting with limited financing forces you to learn every single aspect of the business: how to balance a ledger, how to collect receivables, how to draw up contracts. If you don't understand all aspects of your business, you've set yourself up to fail."*
>
> —*Richard Foos, president, Rhino Records*[6]

Earnings may be taxable

As described earlier in this chapter, under certain circumstances, earnings from nonprofit ventures are subject to unrelated business income taxes (UBIT). In addition to the tax, there may be an administrative burden of tracking taxed versus untaxed sales revenues. Indeed, some nonprofits have a flat policy against *any* unrelated venture income because they don't want to deal with these tax issues.

However, paying income taxes should not be considered a calamity. If your venture gets to the point of paying income taxes, it has achieved profitability, which is worthy of celebration. Some of those after-tax profits will be available to support the nonprofit's activities, which is one of the reasons you went into ventures in the first place.

Do ventures fit with your nonprofit?

Ventures are generally a good "fit" if your nonprofit has

- Support and encouragement for ventures from the leadership
- Adequate flexibility in budget and staff time to allocate to venture activities
- Slow turnover of key personnel
- Ability to make quick decisions
- Recognition of uncertainty and long-term nature of ventures
- Constituents and customers with disposable income

Ventures are likely to be a poor fit if your nonprofit has

- A tight, inflexible budget or an immediate funding crisis
- Overworked and stressed-out staff
- Poor support for ventures from senior staff or board
- Funders, regulators, and other key constituents who would undermine venture efforts
- Low level of innovation, risk-taking, or creativity
- Constituents and customers without much disposable income
- Unrealistic expectations of a quick result

How to Start a Venture

There are many ways to start a venture. Some nonprofits spend months, even years, deciding whether, when, and how to launch one, while others jump in with little more than a hunch. While problems often result from both extremes, most successful ventures begin only after some careful planning has been done. How much planning you need depends on the idea and on your organization.

If your organization already knows a great deal about a venture idea and how its products or services will be valued by customers, and if the start-up costs and risks are low, a shorter planning process is appropriate. Some venture ideas involve relatively simple extensions of current activities. For example, a nonprofit that provides free training may begin charging for the service, provided the participants (or others) seem willing to pay for it, and the costs and risks to turn the activity into a venture are relatively low. The nonprofit might also establish a venture by offering its training activities to a wider customer base for a fee. Starting small with a pilot project that is a simple extension of existing activities can be a great way to learn more about a market, as well as to encourage your organization to operate in a more entrepreneurial manner.

Ventures are not for the weakhearted.

On the other hand, if your nonprofit plans to provide new products or services, or the start-up costs and risks are significant, then success is more likely if you take the time to adequately evaluate the issues before stepping into the competitive marketplace. To take on the risks of a new venture without careful planning would not be prudent.

The venture planning process outlined on these pages is appropriate for a wide range of venture start-ups. Practical suggestions for shaping this process to fit your organization and your venture ideas are noted below.

Time estimates for the venture development process

Typically, it takes six months to a year and at least two hundred hours of work to complete a venture planning process resulting in a business plan for a new venture. If this is your first foray into venture development, two hundred hours may seem like a lot of time; but, in fact, this is a conservative estimate. Most successful nonprofit entrepreneurs, if they actually added up the hours they spent developing a venture, would conclude that this figure was on the low side.

Of course, actual times may vary, depending on your nonprofit's prior venture experience, how your organization makes decisions, and the complexity of the venture ideas you are pursuing. Most managers want to get things going faster, and nearly all end up taking longer.

There's nothing wrong with developing your business plan more quickly, if the circumstances are right, such as if you

- Keep to venture ideas that are simple extensions of what you already do
- Know your target customers and the competition
- Have low start-up costs (including no need for outside financing)
- Hire a consultant with expertise in business development

Below is a summary of the venture development process presented in the rest of this book. Specific details of how to accomplish each step will be presented in the chapters to come.

Minimum times are listed for each step. Some organizations sail through the steps faster than the listed minimums. This is particularly true the second time around. However, most find they need to push themselves to keep on this schedule.

Some organizations want to skip steps if they have already decided on the specific venture idea they wish to evaluate. The steps in the book are flexible enough to allow you to do that, but it's still recommended that you consider many ideas before getting too focused on one. In practice, the first idea is often *not* the best one, which a comparison with other possibilities will demonstrate.

Typically it takes six months to a year and at least two hundred hours of work to evaluate and write a business plan for a new venture.

Of course, actual times may vary, depending on your nonprofit's prior venture experience, how your organization makes decisions, and the complexity of the venture ideas you are pursuing.

Steps of the venture development process

Step 1: Get Organized

Two to four weeks, 8–16 hours

The first step is to organize the venture planning effort. Your organization will select a project leader and venture team to assess how ventures fit with the organization's strategic plan, specify the purpose and overall objectives of ventures for the nonprofit, and secure support from the organization's leadership, including the board of directors. After becoming familiar with the venture planning steps, the team will customize the process and develop a timeline and responsibilities that fit your organization.

Step 2: Conduct a Venture Audit

Three to six weeks, 32–64 hours

This step involves assessing the strengths and weaknesses of your organization for venture development. The venture team will also look for potential customers among current constituents and determine what your organization does best. It is important to identify this information because the best venture opportunities usually build on current constituents and core competencies. This analysis will help determine what kinds of business skills your staff and board of directors possess, and how current constituents and funders will likely respond to proposed ventures. This step also helps you evaluate how much is already known about possible customers, products, and services; and the organization's access to unique products, skill sets, or brand names that would be of interest to those customers.

Step 3: Brainstorm and Screen Venture Ideas

Four to eight weeks, 16–32 hours

At this point, the venture team will decide if outside consulting help is needed, and the executive director will recruit an entrepreneurial committee that includes local business people to challenge and inspire entrepreneurial thinking.

Now the fun begins. The entrepreneurial committee will look over the results of the venture audit, and, keeping those findings in mind, brainstorm venture ideas. Brainstorming will start with the potential customers the nonprofit knows best: your current constituents or others you work with on a regular basis. What unmet needs do they have that match up with your nonprofit's core competencies? Next, the team will think about additional customers and markets to whom you could sell your products or services. After discussing numerous possibilities, the team will narrow the list to the three most promising ideas.

Step 4: Perform Quick Market Tests

Four to eight weeks, 40–80 hours

The venture team will take the three ideas and put them through a quick market test. From written materials and interviews, the team will gather enough external, market-based data to enable it to make a quick judgment on each venture idea. If the results are promising, the team will select one to undergo the more thorough feasibility market research in Step 5. Even if you're looking at just one venture, it's a good idea to use the quick market test to see whether it's sufficiently promising to take it to Step 5.

Step 5: Do Feasibility Market Research

Five to ten weeks, 50–100 hours

Here's where the heavy lifting begins. Feasibility market research, followed by the feasibility financial analysis in Step 6, involves an objective evaluation of a venture idea to determine the likelihood of success and the conditions required to achieve that success. This step takes the most analysis, time, and hard work. It is extremely important, and the failure of nonprofit ventures often can be attributed to inadequate feasibility work. The best venture idea from the previous step is tested against the marketplace by gathering in-depth information on prospective customers, markets, and competitors and comparing that information with the organization's unique strengths and realistic weaknesses. By thoroughly studying the feasibility of a venture idea, you will be able to determine whether you should turn it into a business.

Step 6: Prepare Feasibility Financial Analysis

Three to six weeks, 20–40 hours

This is the point in the feasibility process where the team translates its research into a budget and financial projections, and identifies the remaining uncertainties facing the venture. When this is completed, the organization should have all the information needed to decide whether to launch the venture.

Step 7: Write a Business Plan

Four to eight weeks, 30–60 hours

This step converts the analytical work of the feasibility study (Steps 5 and 6) into a practical implementation plan or, in other words, a business plan. The business plan involves making key decisions about staffing, location, and equipment. It includes specific plans for operations, marketing, and financing. In practice, it takes less time than the feasibility study, but in some ways it is more difficult, requiring tough decisions that will impact what happens when the venture starts up.

As you progress through the venture development process, you may start with an impressionistic, internal perspective based on what you already know. As you consider many venture possibilities, you will move to an external, market-based perspective. Research and analysis will sharpen your focus onto one idea. You will get to know that idea in great detail—as you should, for it will most likely become your new venture.

Seven Steps to a New Venture

Step 1: Get Organized

- Select project leader and venture team
- Clarify why you are pursuing ventures
- Outline a process and timeline that fits your organization
- Decide if additional resources are needed
- Get commitment of key people to proceed

Step 2: Conduct a Venture Audit

- Identify your core customers and core competencies
- Determine your organization's venture capacity
- Anticipate how allies and others will respond

Step 3: Brainstorm and Screen Venture Ideas

- Create an entrepreneurial committee
- Brainstorm venture ideas
- Select three venture ideas for further study

Step 4: Perform Quick Market Tests

- Analyze customers, advantages, and the business model for each venture idea
- Develop research plan for the quick market tests
- Evaluate your ideas; select one for more in-depth feasibility analysis

Step 5: Do Feasibility Market Research

- Develop a feasibility market research plan
- Analyze your customers and competition; identify success factors
- Identify requirements for marketing, operations, pricing, and other factors

Step 6: Prepare Feasibility Financial Analysis

- Create an expense budget and calculate breakeven
- Prepare financial projections and evaluate risks
- Prepare feasibility recommendations

Step 7: Write a Business Plan

- Identify the people who will be in charge and the audience for the plan
- Write the business plan; make final decisions on marketing, operations, and finance
- Get the plan approved

The role of intuition

A note regarding the role of intuition in venture development: Undertaking a complex process such as venture development tends to lead planners down the path of step-by-step, research-based, incremental thinking. To be successful, most businesses need to incorporate that kind of approach into their venture development activities. And certainly, it would be irresponsible to start a venture without first building a solid understanding of why you are taking that action and what the likely consequences will be.

Yet anyone who has worked with small-business owners observes that they do not tend to be step-by-step, research-based, incremental kinds of thinkers. They often act as much on intuition and instincts as they do on analysis—pragmatically jumping from point A to point E if that's what it takes to get the job done. Sometimes they will take that jump despite a lack of data to support it, even against the advice of experts. They are not always right, but it is amazing how often they are.

Most successful entrepreneurs use intuition to bridge the gap between what they know or can find out through research, and what they would like to know in order to make good decisions. Such good business instincts often take years to develop, following extensive experience with both success and failure. Unfortunately, a book may not be the most effective way to acquire that kind of wisdom. This book does offer a reasoned process for approaching venture development, which, in conjunction with the business advice you garner from others, will increase your odds of success.

So, although carrying out the steps outlined on these pages is important and necessary to help your venture get started on the right foot, that will only be sufficient if you also discover ways to supplement the steps with your own intuition backed by personal experience. As you pursue ventures, be sure to go through the steps described in this book, gather the important data identified in each step, and to listen to your intuition and the intuition of others you respect. The business owners on your entrepreneurial committee (Step 3) will be a great resource for this.

As you plan, work, and research your way through this process, also remember how important intuition is to human endeavors. Albert Einstein said,

> *" I believe in intuition and inspiration. At times I feel certain that I am right while not knowing the reason. Imagination is more important than knowledge. For knowlege is limited, whereas imagination embraces the entire world, stimulating progress, giving birth to evolution."* [7]

Most successful entrepreneurs use intuition to bridge the gap between what they know or can find out through research, and what they would like to know in order to make good decisions.

Chapter Two

Prospecting for Ventures

This chapter will help you build a strong foundation for your entrepreneurial project. It shows how and where to look for good venture ideas, by identifying core customers, core competencies, and venture strengths and weaknesses. This information provides the framework for brainstorming business ideas. Finally, this chapter shows how to sift through venture ideas to find the most promising ones.

By the end of Chapter Two, you will have progressed through the first three steps of venture development: Get Organized, Conduct a Venture Audit, and Brainstorm and Screen Venture Ideas. You will have chosen three venture ideas that offer a good fit with your organization. You will analyze these ideas in more detail in Chapter Three.

Step 1: Get Organized
How to get your venture planning effort off on the right foot

Time estimate:

Two to four weeks, 8 to 16 hours of work

Activity summary:

- Select project leader and venture team
- Clarify why you are pursuing ventures
- Outline a process and timeline that fits your organization
- Decide if additional resources are needed
- Get commitment of key people to proceed

The major activity in Step 1 is to organize the work that needs to be done and identify who will do it. The goal is to develop an approach that is both effective (gets the job done) and realistic (can be achieved given available resources). This applies whether you're exploring multiple venture ideas (recommended) or focusing on one.

Project Leader Tasks

❑ Read this book.

❑ Get executive director to select venture team; ask team members to read Chapters One and Two and then scan the rest of the book so they are familiar with the process.

❑ Prepare draft of Venture Objectives (Worksheet 1A) and Process and Timeline (Worksheet 1B).

❑ Discuss objectives and process and timeline with venture team; revise as needed.

❑ Identify and obtain additional resources if needed.

❑ Obtain approvals and proceed to Step 2.

Select project leader and venture team

The first task is to select a project leader, typically someone already on staff, to coordinate and champion the venture development process. This person will be responsible for organizing and coordinating project activities, including gathering internal and external research data and preparing summary reports on venture feasibility. It is important to identify someone with the passion, abilities, and authority to keep things moving forward.[8]

Characteristics to look for in a project leader include

- Action-oriented and results-driven
- Perseverance
- Able to motivate others to act
- Willing to challenge assumptions
- Able to keep meetings on target
- Effective at gathering and organizing information

It is best to select someone from current management—other than the executive director—to serve as the project leader. You want someone who can take a "big-picture" perspective, is respected by other managers, has worked with your board of directors, and can allocate a significant portion of time to this project. A time commitment of ten to twenty hours per week for six months to a year is typical. The amounts vary with the complexity and number of venture ideas to be explored.

Because of the lengthy time commitment, volunteers or interns do not usually work out well as project leaders, although they can help with the legwork. A loaned executive from the private sector or a consultant can take on this responsibility. This works if the person has the right skills (particularly in market research), has experience with nonprofits, and works closely with someone in the nonprofit's leadership who will continue to "own" the project once the executive or consultant moves on. Some organizations select two individuals who work well together to share the project leader role, which reduces disruption of their ongoing responsibilities.

The next task is to select three to five individuals on staff to become the venture team. Their job will be to help the project leader define and carry out the venture development process. The venture team will assist in activities such as gathering data, interviewing sources, preparing reports, and participating in planning meetings.

The venture team should include staff who are most likely to have access to or be familiar with the kinds of information that will be needed to go through the venture process. Individuals who deliver services, who do the accounting, or who are responsible for marketing or outreach would be good for this team. Not every organization has someone in each of these functions, so you will need to adapt to your circumstances. The point is to invite staff with a variety of perspectives in order to broaden the information base. Team members should be able to commit approximately 10 percent of their time to this project.

Read this book. Select venture team; ask team members to read Chapters One and Two and then scan the rest of the book so they are familiar with the process.

Clarify why you are pursuing ventures

The next step on the entrepreneurial journey is to confirm why your organization is interested in venture development. For most nonprofits, the appeal of ventures is the potential to generate sales and earn profits that will lead to reduced dependence on grants and fundraising. As previously noted, some nonprofits also use ventures to help their constituents learn job skills or to provide them with a job.

A third reason is to help your organization expand its entrepreneurial skills and capabilities. For example, surveying your customers to determine their wants and needs, objectively comparing your services with those of your competitors, and developing marketing plans will provide valuable information that your organization can use to evaluate its programs and effectiveness.

Whatever your reason, it will be important to remember that first attempts at ventures often do *not* work out. Ideas need to be tinkered with, revised, or dropped for better ones. Success often comes only after diligently applying the skills and lessons gained from earlier, unsuccessful tries. Entrepreneurship is as much about strengthening the organization as it is about making money. Being explicit that learning as well as earning is important will help you get the most from your venture efforts.

Worksheet 1A: Venture Objectives (page 187) helps the venture team set initial entrepreneurial objectives in three areas—mission, money, and capacity. Agreeing on these objectives will enable management and the board to have a shared understanding of why ventures are being pursued. Organizations that achieve clarity and commitment

Entrepreneurship is as much about strengthening the organization as it is about making money. Being explicit that learning as well as earning is important will help you get the most from your venture efforts.

on these issues *before* they jump into developing ventures are more likely to keep focused and persevere when the inevitable barriers are encountered along the way. A sample Worksheet 1A follows.

At this point in the process, your organization may only be able to articulate general venture objectives. That is perfectly fine; the point is to agree on the initial objectives before going deeply into the process.

Most organizations address mission, money, and capacity in their strategic plan. However, these issues can be discussed separately and do not need to await a formal strategic planning effort. This step does not take a great deal of time, but it does require the focus and attention of your nonprofit's leadership. The important thing is to discuss these issues, put your ideas in written form, and then review them with senior management and the board.

Prepare venture objectives draft.

Feasibility study helps nonprofit uncover its true goals

What nonprofit *doesn't* want to earn more money? The experience of one Pennsylvania senior center shows how the discipline of a feasibility study can help an organization reassess its goals and change strategies. "When we looked at all it would require to set up a business venture, we realized that we didn't have the drive, the champion, the expertise, or the resources to do it. It was healthy to work through the feasibility steps, and to learn that we just couldn't do it with all our other priorities.

If we hadn't tried to find out, we'd still be squabbling," according to the executive director. Now, instead of trying to run a separate business, the organization's board has upgraded its fundraising activities. It is conducting more board-run phonathons and individual solicitations. "Obtaining charitable donations seemed a lot easier after we looked at running a business venture. Who knew this would be the thing that finally got our board fundraising?"[9]

WORKSHEET 1A   Venture Objectives

Instructions

❑ Prepare a draft of Worksheet 1A and Worksheet 1B.

❑ Discuss them with your venture team and the executive director.

❑ Revise as needed.

Example: **Center for Preventing Substance Abuse**

Mission

1. What is your nonprofit's mission? How does the organization carry out that mission?

   To provide information, leadership, and training to prevent substance abuse in our community. We present a variety of workshops on substance abuse issues and maintain a research library of books and publications on the field.

2. Apart from generating income, how do you anticipate that ventures might help you pursue your nonprofit mission?

   We're hoping ventures will help us expand our impact in the community and strengthen relationships with those we currently serve.

Money

3. What amount and percentage of your annual budget currently comes from earned income activities? What are the sources for this income? What is the profit or loss from that income, and how is that measured?

Total budget	**$1 million**
Earned amount	**$60,000**
Earned percent	**6%**

   Sources of earned income are custom training programs, publications, and space rental. Profit is calculated by subtracting direct and indirect costs from sales revenues. Our profit from those activities was approximately $14,000, as indicated on the following chart.

(continued)

	Revenue	Cost	Profit
Custom Training Programs	$30,000	$25,000	$5,000
Publications	$20,000	$20,000	$0
Space Rental	$10,000	$1,000	$9,000
TOTALS	$60,000	$46,000	$14,000

4. In five years, if growth in ventures proves successful, how would you expect these figures to change? A common preliminary target is to increase earned income by ten percentage points.

Estimated total budget in five years   **$1.5 million**

Earned income amount   **$250,000**

Earned income percent   **16.7%**

Capacity

5. Describe how ventures might enhance your organizational skills and capabilities.

- Raise the organization's visibility and reputation

    Depends on the venture. Expanding sales of our publications and custom training would extend our reach.

- Enhance our ability to understand our customers

    Finding out what services people will pay for (and how much they will pay) will help us better understand what they value.

- Expand our ability to analyze program costs and effectiveness

    Our funders are expecting improved measures of outcomes. We're hoping ventures will provide us with some new tools in this area.

- Provide opportunities for staff to build new skills

    Again, depends on the venture. Increased opportunities to improve training and publishing skills would appeal to many of our staff.

(continued)

Worksheet 1A—Venture Objectives

• Other:

> Help us find the right balance between our mission to prevent
> substance abuse, our marketing goals to understand and communi-
> cate to our constituencies, and our business needs to remain fi-
> nancially stable so we can continue addressing our mission.

Concerns

6. What concerns do you have about pursuing ventures? What can you do to address those concerns?

> There is a concern that if ventures are perceived as too suc-
> cessful they may create impression that we don't need other
> support. To address those concerns, we will need to emphasize
> to our funders that ventures are intended to diversify not re-
> place fundraising, and that any profits will be used to support
> the mission.

Outline a process and timeline that fits your organization

The purpose of Step 1 is to identify a process and a set of responsibilities so that everybody knows why your organization is pursuing ventures, who is doing what, and when things will happen. No one magical process applies to every organization, so lay out one that makes sense for your nonprofit. This workbook suggests a seven-step process, but feel free to adapt the information to your needs. As you define your process, be realistic about what can and cannot be accomplished given the experience of key staff and time available to focus on this project. Worksheet 1B: Process and Timeline (page 189) helps you plan and schedule your venture development process. A sample is on page 26.

Prepare draft process and timeline for this project.

WORKSHEET 1B   Process and Timeline

Instructions
- ❑ Prepare a draft process and timeline.
- ❑ Discuss with venture team and executive director.
- ❑ Revise as needed.

Step	Start date	Completion date
1. Get oganized *Present plan to board*	March 1	March 22
2. Conduct a venture audit	March 25	April 15
3. Brainstorm and screen venture ideas *Entrepreneurial committee meeting #1*	April 16	May 20
4. Perform quick market tests *Entrepreneurial committee meeting #2*	May 21	June 27
5. Do feasibility market research *Entrepreneurial committee meeting #3*	July 1	August 14
6. Prepare feasibility financial analysis *Entrepreneurial committee meeting #4* *Present feasibility study to board*	August 15	September 20
7. Write a business plan *Entrepreneurial committee meeting #5* *Present business plan to board*	September 23	November 13

Decide if additional resources are needed

The next task in getting organized is deciding whether you need outside help identifying and evaluating potential venture opportunities. Successful private-sector entrepreneurs are often individuals with highly developed skills in a few areas and sufficient understanding in several more to keep their businesses alive. Most important, they recognize that they cannot be experts at everything. Nonprofit entrepreneurs are no different. They need to objectively determine what the organization does well, what it knows well, and where the gaps are. This helps the nonprofit decide where to apply its energies and when it needs outside expertise.

If outside help is deemed necessary, a variety of resources are available, including books and articles, workshops, colleagues in other nonprofits, and consultants.

- *Books, articles, and web sites.* Bookstores and libraries carry a wide selection of books on entrepreneurship, marketing, and business development. While these books can be helpful, few focus on ventures developed specifically by nonprofits. Publications and web sites that do address this topic can be found in Appendix A and Appendix B. One particularly informative resource is *Enterprising Nonprofits: A Toolkit for Social Entrepreneurs*, by J. Gregory Dees et al.

- *Courses and workshops.* There are a growing number of workshops on starting your own business. Again, few address the unique issues faced by entrepreneurs in the nonprofit world. Nor do they pay attention to the public and community motivations that underpin social entrepreneurship. However, you can still gain valuable business insight from these workshops.

- *Other organizations.* Another source of information consists of nonprofits in your field or geographic area that have been successful with venture development. Find out what they did to succeed and the challenges they faced. Don't be afraid to ask their advice on difficult matters.

- *Consultants.* Some nonprofits use paid or volunteer advisors to help them pursue venture ideas. An experienced and skilled consultant can help keep your effort focused and objectively do the research and analysis. However, someone with a long-term perspective on the organization should remain closely involved. This individual needs to make sure that the plan comes from the organization and is not perceived as the "consultant's plan."

Identify and obtain additional resources if needed.

Get commitment of key people to proceed

Present your venture development plan to other leaders in the organization and to the board to seek their approval. Note that you are seeking approval to commit resources to identify and evaluate venture opportunities. The decision on whether to *launch* any particular venture will come later, following completion of the feasibility analysis and a business plan. Worksheet 1C: Venture Project Approvals (page 190) helps you obtain and track approvals. A sample follows.

Obtain approvals and proceed to Step 2.

WORKSHEET 1C   Venture Project Approvals

Instructions

☐ Complete the following table identifying the members of the venture team, their duties, and the estimated amount of their time that will be needed to work on this project.

☐ Ask each team member to review and initial to confirm their role in the project.

☐ Similarly, request that your executive director approve and sign off on the project objectives of Worksheet 1A and process and timeline of Worksheet 1B.

Venture Project Team Roster:

Title	Name	Project duties	Estimated time	Agreed (initials)
Project leader	Veronica Brown	Everything	33% time 8 months	VB
Team member	Tom Schmidt	Help w/ research	20% time 4 months	TS
Team member	Susan Bentley	Finance	5% time 4 months	SB
Team member	Manuel Chavez	Marketing	10% time 4 months	MC

Venture Project Approvals:

Name	Position	Approved (initials)
Kristine Smathers	Executive director	KS
Jan Euclid	Board chair	JE

Step 1 summary

In Step 1, you organized your venture development effort. You now have a better understanding of how ventures fit within your organization and what you hope to accomplish by pursuing them. You have obtained approval and support from your nonprofit's leadership for the entrepreneurial journey ahead and have identified who will be responsible for doing the actual work.

In Step 2 you will perform an audit of your organization's venture characteristics and take a first look at potential customers.

Step 2: Conduct a Venture Audit
How to do an entrepreneurial assessment of your organization and its potential customers

Time estimate:

Three to six weeks, 32 to 64 hours of work

Activity summary:

- Identify your core customers and core competencies
- Determine your organization's venture capacity
- Anticipate how allies and others will respond

In general, the best venture ideas are those that fit well with your organization. In other words, they build on the relationships, capabilities, and assets that your organization already has. The purpose of the venture audit is to identify your strengths in these three critical areas. This information will then be used in Step 3 to search for venture ideas that take advantage of those strengths.

Note: Before starting this step, read the information at the beginning of the next step about creating an entrepreneurial committee. Forming a committee takes time; so, if your venture timeline is tight, discuss possible committee members with your executive director and invite them to join the committee ASAP.

Venture audit basics

The following three Cs form the basis of a venture audit:

- Core customers
- Core competencies
- Capacity

The first part of the venture audit is to look at your organization's constituents and identify core customers. In most cases, your core customers make the best targets for your venture ideas. You start with your constituents because these are the people and organizations that your nonprofit knows best. Because of your relationship with them, you have, in essence, insider information on what they want and value. You can then use this information to develop venture ideas to address those desires, and to anticipate needs they are not fully aware of yet.

The next part of the venture audit looks at core competencies—what your organization does best. Good venture ideas are an extension of what you already do well because they take advantage of the skills you've developed and knowledge you have in certain areas. Once again, you are taking advantage of insider information—this time on how to do something. Your insider information gives you an edge over the competition and increases your chances of delivering the product or service in a cost-effective way.

The third part of the venture audit focuses on capacity. Here you identify your nonprofit's entrepreneurial characteristics and assets and how they will both help and hinder venture development. Organizations with strong venture skills and good assets can contemplate more challenging venture ideas and look further afield for potential customers.

Project Leader Tasks

❑ Meet with your venture team to discuss your organization's core customers, core competencies, venture capacity, marketable assets, and constituency concerns.

❑ Prepare draft reports in each of these areas (Worksheets 2A through 2E) and review with your venture team.

❑ Present your venture audit, in the form of the completed work-sheets (or a summary of them), to the executive director and board.

A venture idea that makes sense for one organization won't necessarily work for another. Since no nonprofit can possibly be good at everything, acknowledging problem areas can be as important as identifying strengths. In contrast to writing a grant proposal where the underlying purpose is to impress, the venture audit is meant to be a realistic, hard-nosed assessment of your organization. This kind of honesty will help your organization decide what kinds of ventures to pursue and which ones to avoid. If an idea isn't right for your organization or has little chance of success, it's better to know that now, before investing valuable staff time and resources. This kind of self-knowledge also means that you will be playing to your strengths.

Identify your core customers

Every nonprofit has constituents. They are the people and organizations that you serve or that you depend on to succeed. Clients, funders, partners, members, staff, board, and volunteers are all constituents in the sense that they interact with the nonprofit in pursuit of some personal or community need. Constituents provide time, money, or something else they value to the nonprofit in exchange for something they desire.

Your task is to identify which of these constituents are your best prospects to become customers. Many nonprofits assume they cannot sell products or services to their constituents or collect fees from them. When contemplating ventures, they anticipate finding entirely different customers, unrelated to any of their current constituents. The truth of the matter is that although some of your current constituents may not be able to pay, others probably can. Or you may identify groups who are similar to those you currently serve that could be potential customers. Or you may consider whether your specific constituents represent a larger group that you might reach. The point is, broadly consider who your constituents are and which ones have the potential to pay for something you provide or could provide in the future.

Here's a quick example. Breakthrough Urban Ministries, a faith-based urban nonprofit in Chicago, Illinois, that works on homelessness, recognized that the homeless men to whom it provides food and shelter could not be considered prospective customers.[10] By taking a broader perspective, Breakthrough concluded that other constituents—members of evangelical churches and campus groups who provide financial and volunteer support to the nonprofit—could be considered prospective customers.

In looking for potential customers, divide your constituents into smaller groups or segments. Members of a segment share relevant characteristics such as demographics (age, gender, ethnicity), socioeconomics (income, employment), or psychographics (interests, lifestyle, preferences). Establish a division that makes sense for how these constituents use and relate to your organization's products and services. You will need to be specific: "General public" or "business community" is too general. Breakthrough, for example, identified three distinct segments: (1) the Evangelical Free Church, its closest ally; (2) other evangelical churches; and (3) college religious organizations.

The goal is to determine what these segments want and are willing to pay for. Breakthrough found that its contact with the first two segments consisted primarily of high-school-age groups and their parents and church leaders, who were very different in their needs and interests than those of the religious college student segment.

Finally, are there any other prospective customers who are not current constituents, but with whom your organization has a natural link and familiarity, such that you could evaluate what they want and are willing to pay for? If so, there will be place in the next worksheet to list them as well.

Meet with your venture team to discuss your organization's core customers, core competencies, venture capacity, marketable assets, and constituency concerns.

Worksheet 2A: Core Customers on page 191 will help you identify and evaluate your core customers. A sample is on page 32.

WORKSHEET 2A   Core Customers

Instructions

❏ Consider as constituents any community of people or organizations that you now serve.

❏ While it is appropriate to list specific names, try to describe each constituency in terms that could encompass others who are related in some fashion. For example, you could name "Oakdale School District," and expand that to "west metro school districts."

❏ Ignore internal constituents such as staff and board since they are unlikely to become customers for your ventures.

Example: **Center for Preventing Substance Abuse**

1. Who are your constituents? How do they interact with your organization?
   For now, don't worry about overlap between categories.

Constituency	Interaction with your nonprofit and how you provide *value* to *them*
Social workers	Attend our substance abuse (and other) training programs, which provide them with information they can use in their jobs. Also, they earn continuing education unit (CEU) credits from attending our classes, which they need to remain certified (which they need to stay employed as a social worker).
K-12 teachers	Participate in the custom workshops we've developed for teachers, and use the curriculum kits we've developed. Teachers tell us this helps them detect drug abuse and teach the dangers of substance abuse. It also enables them to meet state standards on teaching health issues in the classroom.
School groups	Facilitate workshops on drug use. Increases their awareness of problems with abusing drugs and alcohol. Teachers and parents think the workshops are valuable; less clear is how students see them.
Mental health agencies	We meet their need to keep their staff suitably trained and qualified in techniques and best practices in the substance abuse prevention field.

(continued)

Worksheet 2A—Core Customers

2. What in general do you know about these constituents?
Divide into segments as needed to clarify differences.

Constituency	Overall characteristics (by segment if appropriate)
Social workers	80% female. Advanced degrees (MSW), need 30 CEU credits every two years to retain certification. 8,000 social workers in the state, expected to increase 25% in next three years. Certification training usually selected by social worker and paid for by employer.
K-12 teachers	70% female. Advanced degrees. CEU credits vary by district and area of expertise. Teachers usually pay for their own continuing education, except for occasional workshops that the school district sponsors.
School groups	We get asked most often to do workshops with 5th-9th grade classes. More often suburban rather than urban teachers invite us in.
Mental health agencies	We work with four such agencies: the state and three counties. They have sizable budgets for training.

3. Which of these constituencies or segments represent core customers for your organization? Consider whether you know enough about them to envision products or services that they might want, and whether they are likely to have the ability to pay for such products. Rate on a scale of 1 to 5, where 5 is Yes, 4 is Probably, 3 is Uncertain, 2 is Probably Not, and 1 is No. Why?

Constituency	Core customers?
Social workers	5 - Need CEUs, employer pays for training.
K-12 teachers	3 - Limited employer-paid training funds.
School groups	2 - Very limited dollars available for workshops like ours.
Mental health agencies	4 - They have a strong and continuing interest in the work that we do.

(continued)

4. Finally, are there any other prospective customers who are not current constituents of your nonprofit, but with whom your organization has a natural link and who therefore should be included as you consider new venture possibilities?

Prospective customer	Why? How are we linked to them?
HMOs & insurance companies	Emerging recognition of health benefits and long-term cost savings from prevention and early detection strategies for substance abuse.

Identify your core competencies

Core competencies are your organization's central capabilities that demonstrate your *effectiveness* in pursuing your mission. They are what you do well, what your organization is known for in the community, and what would help you in starting a new program, or a new venture.[11]

There are three tests to determine a core competency:

- Is it something your core customers *value*?
- Is it valued by a *variety* of customer groups?
- Is it difficult for other organizations to imitate?

If the answer is yes to all three, it's a core competency.

Suppose you invited representatives from your various constituencies to a meeting and asked them what words they would use to describe how your nonprofit makes a difference in the community. How would they describe your organization's special contribution? Another way to look at this is to imagine writing a very brief résumé for your organization. Describe your nonprofit's capabilities and accomplishments, using words that would make sense to those you serve.

Most nonprofits possess only a handful of core competencies. Do not be disappointed if you come up with only three or four. Some of the most successful organizations are best known for only one or two things—things that they do incredibly well.

Here are several examples:

Organization	Products/Services	Core competency
Technical school	Classes and degrees	Professional advancement
House of worship	Weekly worship services	Faith-based fellowship and community
Environmental group	Purchase threatened land	Save beautiful places

In each case, recognition of this core competency enabled the organization to better pursue its mission either by attracting new customers or by expanding its relationships with existing ones. Worksheet 2B: Core Competencies (page 193) helps you identify your nonprofit's core competencies. A sample follows.

WORKSHEET 2B   Core Competencies

Instructions

❑ Meet with your venture team to identify how your nonprofit makes a special difference to the community, using words that would make sense to those you serve. Aim for six to twelve possible competencies.

❑ For each competency, list: (1) why your core customers value this; (2) a variety of customers who value or are likely to value this; and (3) why it is difficult for others to imitate.

❑ After the meeting, sift through the list, eliminating or sharpening points that are too general ("quality staff," "good service," "relationship-based"), use insider jargon, or don't meet the three-part core competency test. Then refine and reduce the list down to a manageable number (three or four is best, no more than six) that can be reviewed and approved.

Example: **Southeastern Wisconsin Area Agency on Aging**

Competency: **Expertise on older adult market**

Why your customers value this	Variety of customers who value (or are likely to value) this	Why it is difficult for others to imitate
Confidence that agency understands the needs of older adults	Market research firms, political organizations, and marketers of products targeted at older adults	Unique access to research data concerning older adults; staff expertise interpreting this data; trusted by older adults

Case Study: Hunger relief nonprofit identifies its core competencies[12]

The mission of the Ohio Hunger Task Force (OHTF) is to meet immediate child nutrition needs in the community and to pursue long-term solutions to hunger through advocacy. Its direct service programs include providing daily nutrition to underprivileged children, and its advocacy activities include newsletters, conferences, and press coverage on child nutrition issues.

At a staff meeting, OHTF staff identified four possible core competencies:

- Experience in collecting and communicating childhood nutrition science data
- Ability to mobilize cadres of volunteers
- Knowledge of food distribution logistics
- Ability to form private sector partnerships around childhood nutrition

After further consideration, the staff decided that while all four of these were important capabilities, only two were core competencies. Distribution of childhood nutrition data was important to OHTF's mission, but other nonprofits possessed essentially the same information, and most of it could be found on the Internet or at the local library. Also, while the organization had an active volunteer program, staff members doubted that mobilizing volunteers was one of its unique strengths.

On the other hand, the staff concluded that knowledge of food distribution logistics was a core competency. OHTF's reputation and effectiveness in the community were particularly strong because the nonprofit did more than just talk about nutrition. It was very good at organizing the logistics for providing daily nutrition to 10,000 children.

The second core competency involved the organization's ability to form successful private sector partnerships. It had developed an unusual ability to work constructively with the private sector—particularly the food industry—to address hunger. These partnerships were far more comprehensive and long-term than those maintained by other agencies.

OHTF was able to document that both of these core competencies were highly valued by its key constituents which included schools, families, and community and business leaders. Each of these competencies also suggested possible new venture development opportunities for the organization.

Thus, OHTF decided to define *food distribution logistics* and *private sector partnerships* as the two core competencies it would carry forward into the next phase of its venture development process.

Determine your organization's venture capacity

The third part of the venture audit involves evaluating the general venture development characteristics of your organization. Some nonprofits possess strong internal capabilities to pursue ventures, such as staff and board members with business training and experience, suitable accounting systems, and depth of management. Other nonprofits, particularly smaller, thinly staffed ones or even larger ones that have never charged for services, face obstacles as they contemplate venture development.

When assessing your venture characteristics, you need to consider several categories:

- *Staff continuity*. Frequent staff changes are often incompatible with venture development. A venture needs continuity at both the management and operational level to succeed. Important business relationships—with major customers, suppliers, sales agents, and so on—take time to develop and continuous effort to sustain. Too often ventures go astray because continuity is lost after a key person leaves.

- *Resources.* Financial stability and budget flexibility are just as important as staff continuity. Successful venture development requires a significant commitment of staff time and resources. A reasonable minimal initial commitment would be the ability to assign a staff person to the project for about one-third time for at least six months. In addition, new businesses require start-up money and often need unexpected investments of dollars and staff time. You should contemplate an ambitious venture idea only if your organization can reallocate internal resources or obtain outside funding for this purpose. This may not be practical for small, cash-strapped organizations or nonprofits whose funding will not allow for such reallocation.

  Similarly, social entrepreneurship may not fit well with a nonprofit that suffers frequent financial crises that result in layoffs or severe program cuts. In such cases, absent other sources of funding for venture development, ventures would be a poor investment of scarce management time and financial resources.

- *Experience.* Finally, it is important during this step to evaluate your internal staff capabilities relative to the key skills that help businesses succeed. Do you have managers who are experienced and skilled in understanding, motivating, and supervising the activities of others in a variety of fields, including areas where they themselves might not have extensive experience? Do you have staff with financial expertise who can put together a budget along with income statements and a balance sheet, including notes to these financial statements, in a format that a banker or the entrepreneurial committee would recognize and understand?

Success in ventures is not limited to larger nonprofits, but it is more difficult with small organizations (five or fewer staff). The steps in this workbook presume an organization has the capacity to commit sufficient internal resources to find and evaluate venture ideas and write a business plan for one of those ideas. But smaller nonprofits are not out of the picture altogether; they could consider smaller-scale ventures—those that keep them very close to their core competencies and customers. The techniques in this book would be helpful if the smaller nonprofit were evaluating charging for an existing service, either for current constituents or new customers who are similar to them.

Similar advice applies to larger organizations that receive a low score on Worksheet 2C: Internal Venture Skills. Such organizations might begin to build the requisite experience and flexibility by starting small. Another approach is to find a partner whose strengths correspond to your weaknesses. In the for-profit world, such relationships, known as strategic partnerships, are quite common. Nonprofits often partner with a for-profit company for this reason.

Worksheet 2C: Internal Venture Skills on page 194 will help you answer questions about your nonprofit's venture capacity. A sample is on page 38.

WORKSHEET 2C   Internal Venture Skills

Instructions

❑ Rank each question according to the following scale. (A scoring key appears at the end.)

5 = yes	4 = probably	3 = maybe	2 = probably not	1 = no

Example: **Nature center considering ventures**   **Rating**

1. Do you have the financial stability and budget flexibility to invest sufficient resources (at least one-third full-time employee for six months) into exploring venture opportunities?   **5**

   Explain: **We'll be able to assign staff to this project.**

2. If a promising venture opportunity emerges and a business plan is written, can you invest staff and financial resources into launching that venture?   **4**

   Explain: **The board is on record encouraging more diversified sources of funding, including ventures, and recognizes that it may take an initial investment to launch a new venture.**

3. Do you have strong financial and accounting capability on staff?   **4**

   Explain: **Our accounting systems are very strong for the reporting we currently need to manage the nonprofit and to satisfy funder requirements. Some changes may be needed to do venture accounting, however, depending on the venture idea.**

4. Do you have strong financial and accounting capability on the board?   **4**

   Explain: **Finance committee now includes a former bank executive.**

5. Do you have strong marketing background and experience on staff?   **4**

   Explain: **We have an excellent in-house promotions staff and good marketing for our programs. Not sure how the program marketing experience would translate to venture marketing, however.**

6. Do you have strong marketing background and experience on the board?   **3**

   Explain: **A board member with a marketing background recently rotated off the board. However, this ex-board member has expressed continuing interest in helping us developing a venture.**

(continued)

Worksheet 2C—Internal Venture Skills

	Rating

7. Do you have staff stability and continuity (slow turnover), especially for the three most senior positions in the organization?   **4**

   Explain: **Two of the top three have been around for five or more years.**

8. Does your organizational culture encourage innovation, risk taking, and long-term thinking?   **3**

   Explain: **We have a history of innovative programs—not sure how that interest would translate to business ventures.**

9. Do the executive director and the board support the development of earned income ventures?   **4**

   Explain: **Topic has come up at board meetings during funding discussions; both executive director and board have expressed interest.**

10. Do you have a solid internal cost-accounting system that provides reliable data on fixed and variable costs for each program or activity?   **4**

    Explain: **Our budget system is good at allocating expenses between programs, but does not distinguish fixed from variable costs.**

11. Do you have the ability to establish the cost for a unit of service?   **4**

    Explain: **Yes, provided we can define (and agree on) a unit of service. Our cost data is very good.**

Total score   **43**

SCORING   <33 Weak   34–38 Fair   39–43 Good   44+ Excellent

Identify your unique, marketable assets

Many nonprofits own assets that could be used for commercial advantage. These assets can be tangible or intangible. Tangible assets include real estate, equipment, and vehicles. Intangible assets include reputation, brands, and intellectual property. To be useful for a venture, an asset has to be valued by the marketplace.

Many nonprofits are thinking creatively about how to make money from their tangible assets. For example, a zoo or museum may make certain areas of its building available for public parties and receptions; a public radio station may lease space on its transmission tower to a cellular phone company; an urban church may rent out its parking lot during weekdays.

Many assets are intangible, in that they lack a physical presence. A brand such as The Whopper or Post-it Notes is essentially a promise to deliver a product or service with consistency no matter where you find it. Burger King and 3M, the owners of these popular brands, possess intangible assets valued by millions of customers.

For many nonprofits, a significant intangible asset is their reputation. It could be a reputation for reliability, service quality, or skilled staff. You must determine if there are prospective customers who would find that reputation sufficiently valuable to influence their buying decisions. This is the logic behind affinity credit cards, where a nonprofit gets a fee every time someone signs up for and uses a credit card that bears its logo.

Nonprofits often have a reputation for trustworthiness. In recent years, some energy companies have relied on nonprofits to certify that some energy they produce is environmentally friendly or "green." Why? Because a large energy company understands that customers interested in cleaner energy are more likely to believe the company's claims if the energy product has the blessing of an environmental group whose name they trust.

Another intangible asset is intellectual property. This includes proprietary procedures and content, such as copyrighted training materials, published materials, databases, patents, proprietary software, and specialized skills in management and service delivery.

Use Worksheet 2D: Marketable Assets on page 196 to brainstorm and record your list of tangible and intangible assets. A sample is on page 41.

Anticipate how allies and others will respond

Since most nonprofits obtain the lion's share of their budget from contributions and grants, it is important to anticipate the response of funders and other constituents. While some funders encourage efforts to diversify funding sources, even agreeing to

---

Many nonprofits own assets that could be used for commercial advantage. Tangible assets include real estate, equipment, and vehicles; intangible assets include reputation, brands, and intellectual property.

WORKSHEET 2D   Marketable Assets

Instructions
- ❑ With help from the venture team, mentally browse through your organization, looking for tangible and intangible assets that are valued or might be valued by paying customers.
- ❑ Discuss each asset, and decide which ones show enough potential to be placed on the worksheet.

Asset	Potential customers	Why they might be interested and willing to pay
Example: Computer-based training facility and conference space	Corporate training and conferences	Convenient offsite location for nearby businesses
Example: Church parking lot	Adjacent retail businesses	Overflow for weekday and Saturday shoppers

help fund ventures, others shy away from it. Some organizations funded almost entirely by government are flatly prohibited from earning outside income or, in rare cases, are even required to return to the funder every dollar earned from such activities.

Would any of your key constituent organizations oppose your efforts to engage in venture development? In addition to funders, there might be other nonprofits or private companies who would object. An example of this would be a nonprofit whose board is made up of representatives from other organizations that might oppose your entry into activities that compete with them. Some level of concern is almost always raised by at least one constituent group, so it's good to think about this early. Worksheet 2E: Constituency Concerns, on page 197 will help you anticipate these responses.

Finally, it's worth taking a moment to explore whether nonconstituent organizations might object to your pursuit of venture income sources. Of course, this often depends on what kind of venture you start. In any event, if you are aware of someone who may object to your venture plans, now is the time to anticipate that reaction. In rare cases such objections can force nonprofits to forego a specific venture; more often the increased awareness helps the nonprofit take steps to prevent a major problem.

Worksheet 2E helps you anticipate responses from your key constituency groups. A sample is on page 42. You may want to answer the questions again when you have narrowed your prospective venture ideas to the most promising ones.

WORKSHEET 2E   Constituency Concerns

Instructions

❑ The executive director is probably the best person to address constituency concerns. Discuss this worksheet with him or her, and then fill out a summary.

Example: **Services to individuals with mental illness**

Funders

1. Who are your most important funders?

   State and county government, several local foundations, corporate sponsors.

2. How do you anticipate that each would respond if your organization decides to set up a venture? Would it matter what kind of a venture?

   We expect our foundation and corporate funders to be supportive or neutral. We anticipate less enthusiasm from government, particularly the county, which accounts for 80%+ of our budget. Their policies prohibit charging fees for any services they fund, even in part. We won't use funds we receive from them to develop ventures, but they still might object. At times they treat us as if we were a state agency, so we'll need to address this one carefully.

Board

3. How will your board react?

   Our board is VERY enthusiastic about ventures, mostly with the hope that they will decrease our dependence on county government for funding (which limits the kinds of services and populations we can serve). Two board members were the initial catalyst for this effort.

Allies

4. How about key nonprofit allies—are there any that would challenge your decision to launch a venture? Would that represent a threat to your organization?

   None that we are aware of.

Rivals

5. Are there nonprofit or for-profit rivals that could also challenge such a decision? Would that represent a threat?

   Will depend on the specific venture idea developed; we must revisit this question when that has been determined. We are worried that organizations competing with us for government funds will "suggest" that with our ventures we won't need as much funding.

Prepare draft reports in each of these areas (Worksheets 2A through 2E) and review with your venture team. Present your venture audit, in the form of the completed worksheets (or a summary of them), to the executive director and board.

Step 2 summary

After completing Step 2, you should have a clear idea of your organization's customers, competencies, venture capacities, and marketable assets. The internal venture skills and constituency concerns worksheets indicate the types of ventures and the level of risk appropriate for your organization. All of the information collected in Step 2 will provide the framework for the next step of brainstorming and screening venture ideas.

Step 3: Brainstorm and Screen Venture Ideas
Where to look for promising venture ideas

Time estimate:

Four to eight weeks, 16 to 32 hours of work

Activity summary:

- Create an entrepreneurial committee
- Brainstorm venture ideas
- Select three venture ideas for further study

Using the venture audit as a springboard, this step describes how to look for venture ideas that build on your organization's unique characteristics. It begins by creating a committee that includes local businesspeople who will help bring an entrepreneurial mind-set to the project.

There are two parts to the work in this step: brainstorming and screening. Brainstorming is generating venture ideas that would use your organization's competencies, capacity, and marketable assets to deliver products or services to the customer groups identified in the venture audit. Screening is narrowing your long list of brainstormed ideas to a manageable number.

By the end of this step, you will have chosen three promising venture ideas that you will then research in Step 4.

Project Leader Tasks

❑ Recruit entrepreneurial committee and schedule initial meeting; send committee members the agenda, your venture audit, the Venture Brainstorming Pyramid (page 46), and suggested brainstorming guidelines (page 45). Ask them to jot down venture ideas.

❑ Convene initial entrepreneurial committee meeting to discuss venture audit and to brainstorm venture ideas.

❑ Develop a set of criteria on which to rank the venture ideas. Send the list of venture ideas and the screening criteria to the venture team and the entrepreneurial committee; ask them to rank the ventures according to the criteria.

❑ According to the ranking, choose the three best ideas for further analysis.

Create an entrepreneurial committee

The first action to take in Step 3 is for your executive director to recruit an entrepreneurial committee to help guide and inspire the project. The committee will review the venture audit, take part in brainstorming, be available for advice during the feasibility testing, and, ultimately, review findings and make recommendations to the board. Committee members have a very important role, and nonprofits contemplating ventures for the first time find their involvement helps to jump-start the nonprofit's venture efforts. Entrepreneurial committees are very good at challenging your assumptions and pushing your nonprofit in new and valuable directions.[13]

An entrepreneurial committee typically consists of seven to eleven individuals that include

- Two board members (one of them should chair the committee)
- Two to four successful entrepreneurs who are not currently board members (they do not need to be familiar with your organization)
- The executive director, project leader, and the venture team
- A consultant, if you have hired one for this project

Recruit entrepreneurial committee and schedule initial meeting; send committee members the agenda, your venture audit, the Venture Brainstorming Pyramid, and suggested brainstorming guidelines. Ask them jot down venture ideas.

Brainstorm venture ideas

The major purpose of the first meeting of your entrepreneurial committee is to solicit venture ideas. Getting committee members to brainstorm is usually quite easy; people love to offer suggestions *they* don't have to implement. Some of their venture ideas will be good, while others will be impractical. In the spirit of brainstorming, consider each idea a special contribution to the process and move on to the next one. Later on you'll narrow the list to a more manageable number.

Here's a suggested agenda for the meeting, with the person guiding the discussion in parentheses. Be sure to allot at least two and preferably three hours for this meeting.

- Welcome and introductions (Chair)
- What is venture development? Why are we doing this? (Executive director)

- Role of the entrepreneurial committee (Chair)
- Overview of the venture development process (Project leader)
- Review and critique of the venture audit (Executive director)
- Brainstorming venture ideas (Project leader)
- Wrap-up, set date for next meeting (Project leader)

A few suggestions for the brainstorming part of the agenda:

- *Allow enough time.* Reserve at least ninety minutes for brainstorming. Discuss and agree on the guidelines for brainstorming (see box at right) before the brainstorming begins.

- *Set the context.* Explain that the search is for venture ideas that build on your venture audit results. Such venture ideas will deliver products or services to the prospective customers identified in Worksheet 2A, or build on your core competencies and other capabilities (Worksheets 2B through 2D), or, best yet, do both.

- *Use the Venture Brainstorming Pyramid.* This figure, found on page 46, graphically underscores the point that the best venture ideas are those closest to the organization's existing customers—those at or near the bottom of the pyramid. The higher you go on the pyramid, the greater the risk and difficulty your venture will have in succeeding. While the spirit of brainstorming allows for all types of ideas, the job of the project leader is to make sure there are enough ideas from the base of the pyramid.

- *Focus the discussion and collect ideas.* Use Worksheet 3A: Brainstorming Venture Ideas on page 198. (A sample appears on page 47.) Take each prospective customer from Worksheet 2A and ask the committee to suggest products or services that reflect your core competencies and that the nonprofit could deliver to this customer group. Ask committee members to suggest what benefits these customers would get from these products or services. Be sure to indicate that venture ideas higher up on the pyramid are still welcome, as long as the group builds a solid base of venture ideas from the bottom two sections.

- *Consider business-to-business ventures.* Finally, encourage the committee to consider services to other organizations (nonprofit, for-profit, or government) in addition to sales directly to consumers. This area, known as the business-to-business market, might open up some new possibilities. For example, a welfare-to-work and employment readiness program might develop a complete training package for sale to school districts, business associations, and state agencies.

Convene initial entrepreneurial committee meeting to discuss the venture audit and to brainstorm venture ideas.

Suggested guidelines for brainstorming venture ideas

- Everyone's ideas are encouraged (some of the best ones come from unexpected sources).
- *Every* suggestion is welcome—no matter how unclear, outlandish, or impractical.
- Avoid evaluating or judging ideas, which can halt the flow. This will come later.
- Build on each other's ideas; any suggestion can become the seed of another idea.
- Have fun with it! It's okay to be silly or extreme; often the best ideas emerge when you least expect them.
- Keep a time limit on each idea—ten minutes maximum.
- When you think you are done, review the list. Connections may be made as the group reviews the list of ideas.

Figure 1. Venture Brainstorming Pyramid

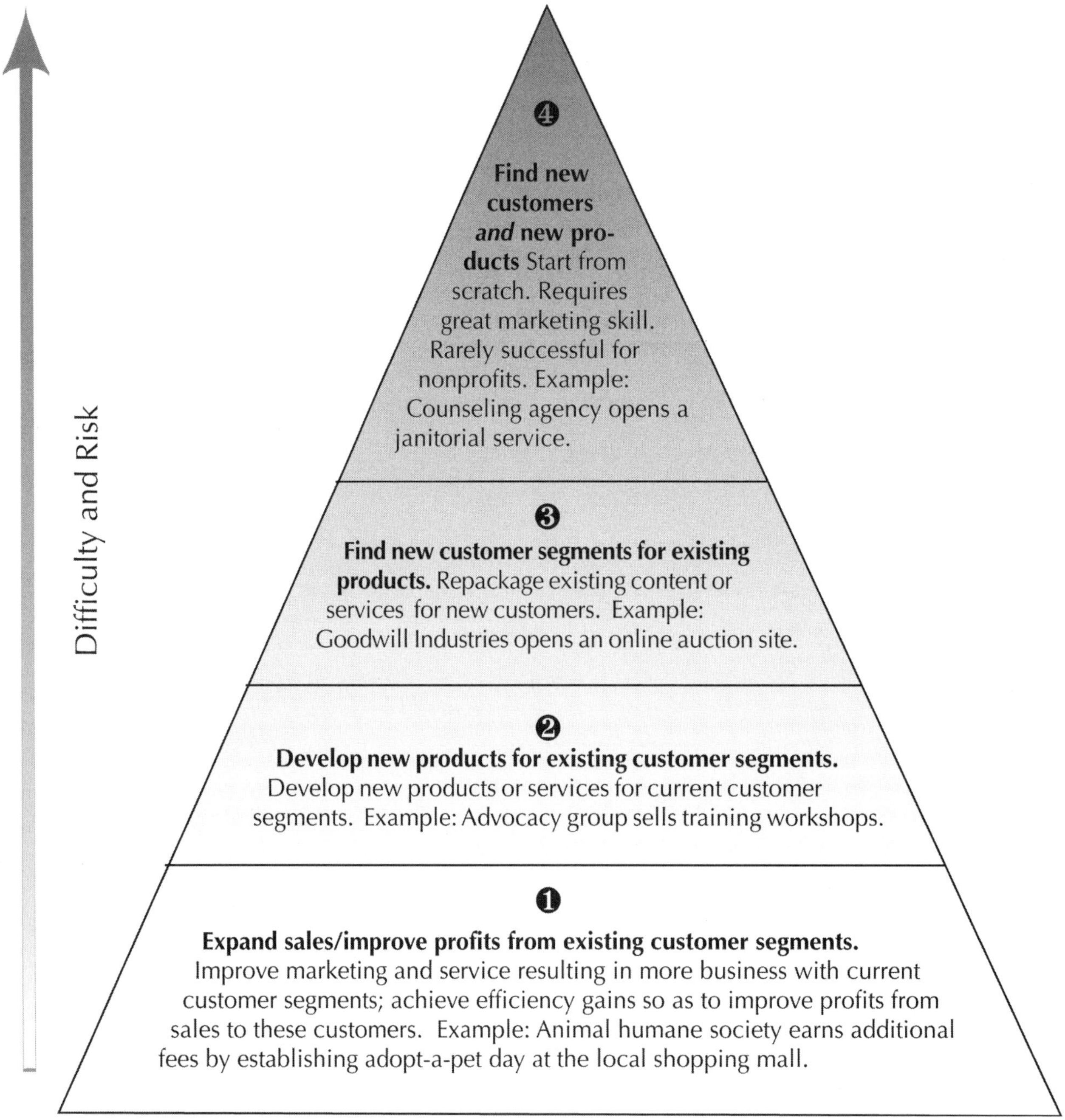

Difficulty and Risk

❹

Find new customers *and* new products Start from scratch. Requires great marketing skill. Rarely successful for nonprofits. Example: Counseling agency opens a janitorial service.

❸

Find new customer segments for existing products. Repackage existing content or services for new customers. Example: Goodwill Industries opens an online auction site.

❷

Develop new products for existing customer segments. Develop new products or services for current customer segments. Example: Advocacy group sells training workshops.

❶

Expand sales/improve profits from existing customer segments. Improve marketing and service resulting in more business with current customer segments; achieve efficiency gains so as to improve profits from sales to these customers. Example: Animal humane society earns additional fees by establishing adopt-a-pet day at the local shopping mall.

WORKSHEET 3A   Brainstorming Venture Ideas

Instructions

❏ At the entrepreneurial committee meeting, review the venture audit, Venture Brainstorming Pyramid (page 46), and brainstorming guidelines (page 45).

❏ Emphasize that while the goal is to look for venture ideas that would build on your audit strengths, all ideas are welcome.

❏ Ask that ideas indicate customer group, product or service idea, and likely customer benefits. (See chart below.)

❏ Write down each of the brainstormed ideas including target customers. Refer to the pyramid to make sure most of the ideas come from the bottom half.

❏ After the meeting, the project leader should write up the list, rewording vague ideas and eliminating clearly impractical ones.

Example: **Urban counseling service**

Customer group	Product or service ideas	Customer benefits
Older adults	1. Financial planning for older women	1. Gain control over your money
	2. Sensitive, safe dating service	2. Companionship
	3. Health club with special equipment	3. Exercise safely to promote health
	4. Elder home care service	4. Provide non-medical care
Families	1. Day care for night-shift parents	1. Ease of mind
	2. Counseling for divorcing parents	2. Reduce impact on children
	3. Workshops for "blended" families	3. Simple strategies for complex families
	4. Crisis day care services	4. Relief
Schools	1. Nonviolence and gang prevention services	1. Early prevention
	2. Special education evaluations	2. Measure program effectiveness

Select three ideas for further study

If you're like most organizations at this point in the process, you have a long list of possible venture ideas. But don't worry if your list is short. Quality is more important than quantity. In Step 4 you will market-test the ideas. Since it's just not practical to gather market data on more than a handful of these venture ideas, you need to winnow the list to the three most promising ideas.

The first part of screening the list is to "polish it." The project leader should combine, edit, and clarify the venture ideas on Worksheet 3A so there is one clean summary of the ideas under consideration. Write up each venture idea as a brief description, being sure to indicate the idea, the likely customers, and the benefit to customers.

The second part of screening it is to establish a set of criteria on which to rank these venture ideas. The following is an example of criteria an organization might use to narrow the list to no more than three venture ideas. Feel free to develop criteria that fit your situation.

Strategic fit? Does this venture fit with our mission and strategic plan?

Core competency fit? Will it build on our core competencies and other capabilities?

Expand core competencies? Will this venture help us build valuable new core competencies?

Core customer fit? Does it involve some of our core customers or others just like them?

Will customers pay? Does it seem likely that customers will be willing to pay for this?

Profit potential? Does this seem like it has the potential to generate profits?

Use Worksheet 3B: Screening Chart (page 199) to list the venture ideas and your criteria; then distribute it to your venture team and entrepreneurial committee along with a cover note that indicates when you need their replies. A sample follows.

 Develop a set of criteria on which to rank the venture ideas. Send the criteria and the venture ideas to the venture team and the entrepreneurial committee; ask them to use the criteria to rank the ventures.

WORSHEET 3B   Screening Chart

Instructions

❑ Create a summary table similar to the one below, along with additional notes on an attached page if necessary to explain the concept.

❑ Present the list to your venture team and the entrepreneurial committee to solicit their votes.

❑ Tally up the votes, and lead a discussion at a second entrepreneurial committee meeting on what the numbers suggest, and where they may be off the mark.

❑ At that meeting, or subsequently with the venture team, select no more than three venture ideas to undergo the quick market test.

❑ Rank each venture according to the following scale.

| 5 = yes | 4 = probably | 3 = maybe | 2 = probably not | 1 = no |

Example: **Urban counseling service**

Venture Idea	Criteria						
	Strategic fit?	Core comp fit?	Expand core comps?	Core customer fit?	Will customers pay?	Profit potential?	Total
On-site day care for night-shift workers	4	5	3	2	3	1	18
Older adult health club	2	2	4	5	3	3	19
Elder home care services	5	4	5	5	4	3	26

When you have received the completed screening charts, tally the votes for each venture idea. Then convene a second entrepreneurial committee meeting and present the results. Lead a discussion on what the numbers suggest and where they may be off the mark. At that meeting, or subsequently with the venture team, select no more than three venture ideas to undergo the quick market test.

Choose the three best venture development ideas for further analysis in Step 4.

Step 3 summary

In Step 3, you recruited an entrepreneurial committee and involved the members in brainstorming a list of venture ideas and in narrowing that list down to the best three. In Step 4 you will test those ideas to see which one has the best potential for your organization.

Chapter Two Summary

With help from your venture team and your entrepreneurial committee, your non-profit has come a long way in the venture development process. During the first three steps, you became organized, completed a venture audit, brainstormed venture ideas, and then chose three ideas for further consideration. Your decisions up to now have been based on what you already know.

In Chapter Three you will evaluate those three ideas based on externally gathered market research and analysis. Using this information, you will confirm or update your impressions of those venture ideas, determine which idea is best, and then decide if it represents a worthwhile venture opportunity. Chapter Four describes how to write a business plan to turn such an idea into a successful, operating business.

Chapter Three

Testing the Feasibility of Your Venture Ideas

Now that you have identified three promising venture ideas, it's time to test them against the marketplace through research and analysis. Feasibility testing separates true opportunities from mere ideas. A venture idea may sound promising, but until you've researched the market, thoroughly looked at customer preferences, compared your product to competitors' products, and determined the requirements for success in marketing, operations, and finance, you won't be able to say with confidence "this venture will succeed." If your idea is a good one, feasibility testing will give you that confidence.

By the end of this chapter you will have researched and analyzed your venture ideas in sufficient detail to decide if you should turn one of them into a business. If the answer is yes, then Chapter Four will show you how to prepare a business plan to start it up.

Feasibility testing refers to evaluating whether a venture is likely to succeed. This is accomplished through market research that identifies the venture's requirements for success and predicts its likely financial results. Requirements are characteristics that your venture must possess in order to attract paying customers and earn profits, such as staff skills, special equipment, or specific marketing capabilities. For example, a non-profit researching the idea of providing continuing education classes to nurses might deem certification from nursing accreditation organizations as a requirement.

The purpose of market research is, first, to test the information and impressions you already have about this venture idea and, second, to fill in any gaps in your knowledge. Market research may happily confirm your information, but you may also find that some of it needs to be revised and updated. Nonprofit managers typically focus on community needs. As a business manager, you will focus more on what customers want and are willing to pay for.

If feasibility testing gives a thumbs-up to the venture idea, then writing a business plan to launch the business is the next step. The business plan describes how your organization will satisfy the requirements identified during feasibility testing. In other words, the business plan provides the specifics on who, what, where, and how the venture will operate to be successful. For example, if feasibility testing demonstrated that a certain type of building and a manager with industry experience would be needed for this venture to succeed, then the business plan would identify the location of the building that will be used and the individual who will be running the venture. Feasibility testing is about evaluation; a business plan is about implementation. The good news is that thorough feasibility testing provides 75 percent of the information you will need to complete a business plan.

Some people use the term *business plan* to encompass both evaluation and implementation. Others refer to financial projections (and little else) as their business plan. In this book, the two concepts of feasibility testing and writing a business plan are separated; if an idea proves not to be feasible, you can save yourself the time of writing a business plan.

Feasibility testing involves considerable time and hard work. To make the work more manageable, this book divides the process into three steps: a quick market test (Step 4) to gather sufficient data to select the best venture idea from the three you've been considering; feasibility market research (Step 5) for a full analysis of that idea; and feasibility financial analysis (Step 6) to run the numbers on that idea.

Some organizations may not have gone through Steps 1 through 3 and are simply considering a "hot" idea as a possible venture. If this is your situation, it's still a good idea to put the idea through a quick market test to help decide whether it's worth the investment of time to go through Steps 5 and 6.

Step 4: Perform Quick Market Tests

How to gather preliminary market data to decide which is the most promising venture idea

Time estimate:

Four to eight weeks, 40 to 80 hours of work

Activity summary:

- Analyze product, customers, advantages, and the business model for each venture idea
- Develop a research plan for the quick market tests
- Evaluate your ideas; select one for more in-depth feasibility analysis

By the end of this step, you will have narrowed your focus to the most promising venture idea, in preparation for the in-depth market analysis of Step 5.

The purpose of a quick market test (QMT) is to gather sufficient external, market-based data to enable you to make a quick judgment on each of your three venture ideas. You do this by talking to potential customers and to those who know something about them, and by spending time in the library or at your computer. A quick market test is sometimes referred to as a preliminary feasibility test.

A typical quick market test takes about twenty hours of staff time per venture idea, spread out across several weeks to allow enough time to collect data and conduct interviews. If you do several quick market tests concurrently, you should be able to complete work on all of them in four to eight weeks.

Analyze product, customers, advantages, and the business model for each venture idea

A quick market test has the following four components, which make up the abbreviation PCAM:

- **P**roduct—A clear description of the proposed product or service

- **C**ustomers—Identification of the customers and markets where this product would be sold

- **A**dvantages—Unique or unusual advantages your organization possesses that will make a difference to those customers and markets

- **M**odel—The business model that describes how you will make money from this venture

Project Leader Tasks

❏ Read all of Chapter Three.

❏ Draft answers to those Worksheet 4A: QMT Twenty Questions that you already have information on.

❏ Prepare an outline of your Worksheet 4B: QMT Research Plan.

❏ Discuss QMT research plan with venture team. Delegate research duties. Agree on expectations and timetable. Send to entrepreneurial committee for suggestions and contacts.

❏ Complete the final QMT Twenty Questions (Worksheet 4A) and Scorecard (Worksheet 4C).

❏ Present your results (Worksheets 4A and 4C) first to the venture team and your executive director, and then to the entrepreneurial committee.

❏ If the decision is made that your findings support proceeding to feasibility market research (Step 5), solicit the entrepreneurial committee's advice and contacts to accomplish this.

Worksheet 4A: QMT Twenty Questions on page 200 presents questions in these four categories. Fill in the information you already know for each question. A sample is on page 54.

Read all of Chapter Three. Draft answers to those QMT Twenty Questions that you already have information on.

WORKSHEET 4A   Quick Market Test Twenty Questions

Instructions

❏ Use a separate worksheet for each venture idea.

❏ Answer as many questions as you can with available information; then design a QMT research plan (Worksheet 4B) to fill in gaps and verify your information.

❏ Based on your research findings, complete this worksheet.

Name of venture: **Provident Counseling**[14]

Product

1. Clearly describe the proposed product or service.

   Eldercare Services—Housekeeping and personal care services provided at home to elderly adults.

2. How will you produce and deliver it?

   Contract with qualified individuals for services such as housekeeping, chores, and home maintenance; contract with nursing assistants for care needs such as bathing, laundry, and light cooking.

3. How will customers find it beneficial to them?

   Elderly adults often need special health, social, and personal care services due to physical or mental limitations. Top priority for most elderly adults is to remain in their homes. This service helps them remain independent in a convenient and trusted manner.

Customers

4. Who are your target customers?

   Elderly adults and their caregivers. The caregivers are often middle-aged "sandwich-generation" adults, employed people with children at home to be cared for who also feel responsible for the well-being of their elderly parents. This service would offer convenience and confidence that their elderly parents were receiving the care they needed.

5. What relationship do you have with your target customers?

   Our organization has provided a variety of counseling services to the community for over 50 years and our client mix includes middle-aged and older adults. Through our employee assistance programs, we already provide services to many working "sandwich-generation" adults.

(continued)

6. What evidence do you have of customer interest?

   `Independent living and care giving issues for older adults often`
   `emerge from counseling; also, employers ask about this.`

7. How will you sell this product to these customers?

   `Access will be obtained via corporate employee assistance programs`
   `(EAP), through elderly apartment complexes, and through senior`
   `centers. We currently provide EAP counseling services to 30 local`
   `companies, covering 40,000 employees, so we already know the EAP`
   `market.`

8. Are they growing in numbers or buying more each year?

   `The 85+ age group is growing three to four times faster than the`
   `general population. By the year 2030, one in five adults will be 65`
   `or older, doubling the number of older Americans. About one-third`
   `of noninstitutionalized older adults currently live alone; almost`
   `half of older women are widows. The at-home "frail elderly" are of`
   `special concern, and represents a special opportunity for a ser-`
   `vice like this.`

9. What is important to these customers?

   `Confidence that the service will be delivered by trustworthy,`
   `reliable, skilled people who, ideally, do not vary from one visit`
   `to the next.`

Advantages

10. How does this venture build on your core competencies?

    `We specialize in flexible, professional, and personalized social`
    `services, which is precisely what this venture requires.`

11. How will you produce and deliver this product efficiently?

    `We'll hire home health aides, nursing assistants, and others on a`
    `part-time basis to deliver the services. We'll provide supervision`
    `and training as needed.`

(continued)

Worksheet 4A—Quick Market Test Twenty Questions

12. What is the competition for this product?

> Under Home Health Services in the Yellow Pages, we noticed several possible competitors, including Home Instead, which seems to offer a service similar to what we're proposing.

13. How difficult would it be for another firm to replicate your product?

> Entry to this market would be relatively easy, as this is a labor-intensive service requiring relatively low initial capital outlays.

14. Why would customers prefer your product?

> We have strong name recognition within the community, especially in government social service circles, in major corporations in town, and in the media. This will help us get good publicity and referrals for our service. Customers will prefer our service either because of this name recognition or because of a referral from someone or an organization they trust.

15. How does this idea fit with your mission and the attitude of key stakeholders?

> Mission fit is good; unsure how our stakeholders will respond if we enter this venture area.

Business Model

16. What evidence do you have that customers will pay for this and that there is profit potential?

> We discovered several competitors that have been in business for at least five years (per call to the Secretary of State's office). We interviewed a couple of human resource directors of major companies in town who indicated that employees often ask whether services like this exist. No evidence so far on profit potential.

17. What are the start-up costs for this venture and where will the funding come from?

> Mostly administrative and marketing in nature, the costs do not seem prohibitive at the moment. Could probably use our existing office facilities to coordinate this service.

18. What is the minimum sales level needed to make a profit?

> Unclear at this point, but does not seem to be prohibitively high.

(continued)

Worksheet 4A—Quick Market Test Twenty Questions

19. What weaknesses will your nonprofit face in running this venture?

> `Liability risk (miscommunication or error leads to failure to de-`
> `liver service, which adversely impacts the elderly client); service`
> `providers prove unreliable or a constantly changing staff so clients`
> `lose comfort and trust in service. We have experience delivering`
> `services in a corporate or office setting; delivering services in a`
> `home setting will be something new.`

20. What staff (both managerial and operational) will you need to operate this venture?

> `Initially a current staff person would manage the launch of this ven-`
> `ture. Additionally, we will need a manager on-call during evening and`
> `night hours. We'll contract with qualified individuals (housekeepers,`
> `home health aides, nursing assistants) to deliver the services.`

Develop a research plan for the quick market tests

The next task is to design a QMT research plan for gathering additional market-based data to complete the QMT Twenty Questions worksheet. This research involves gathering information from three types of sources:

1. *Written* material from books, newspapers, trade associations and the industry press, government publications, and magazines. Tips for using the Internet to gather data appear in the sidebar "Tips for Internet-assisted research" on page 61. A list of general web sites for doing Internet research appears in Appendix C.

2. *Oral* interviews with individuals who have specialized knowledge and can shed light on the products, industry, and markets under consideration. Examples include potential customers, industry association spokespersons, distributors, suppliers, trade journalists, and government officials. Surprisingly, people in the industry are often willing to share their experiences with you, especially if for geographic or other reasons you won't be competing with them. Nonprofits are often willing to share information despite the possibility of new competition. The sidebar "Interviewing tips" on page 64 contains useful suggestions for conducting interviews.

3. *Secret shopping* at your competitors' business operations. Either you or a colleague pose as a customer interested in their products. Secret shopping works for both consumer and business-to-business ventures. Collect brochures, and visit the facility, even purchase something to see how they treat their customers.

It may seem difficult to know where to locate information for the quick market test, but in practice it's not that hard. Assuming that your venture ideas build on your organization's core competencies, market knowledge, and experience, you and others in your organization will already be familiar with many information sources. The entrepreneurial committee should also be a good source for referrals. Finally, consider whether you know anyone else who might offer some perspective on the QMT questions: your neighbor, a cousin, a business where you are a customer, and so on. Be creative.

Typically, sufficient information for most quick market tests can be obtained from interviewing three to five people and spending five to ten hours gathering written data. Figure 2 on page 59 presents examples of where nonprofits have obtained research information for their quick market tests.

 Prepare an outline of your QMT research plan. Discuss QMT research plan with venture team. Delegate research duties. Agree on expectations and timetable. Send to entrepreneurial committee for suggestions and contacts.

Worksheet 4B: QMT Research Plan on page 203 will help you plan your work. A sample is on page 60. Remember, you only have about twenty hours to spend per venture idea, so keep the work focused.

Buy rather than build?

It is not always necessary to start a venture from scratch. While the conventional entrepreneurial approach is to *build* a business from the ground up, an alternative and often speedier technique is to *buy* your way into a business. One way to buy rather than build is to acquire an existing business, one whose experience and reputation enable your organization to save the costs, time, and risks required to develop venture capabilities. For example, a nonprofit considering a venture running focus groups might decide that it would be more practical to purchase a small marketing firm already in that business. While it is beyond the scope of this book to provide advice on buying a business, it's an alternative you should remain open to while evaluating venture possibilities.

A second way to buy rather than build is through a franchise arrangement. One advantage of buying into a successful franchise is that operations and marketing strategies have already been worked out. One nonprofit decided that its best venture idea was to purchase a Mail Boxes Etc franchise.

Finally, a nonprofit could decide to outsource a venture. Many colleges, for example, are outsourcing their bookstores to private firms, generating a royalty from what previously was a losing proposition.

Figure 2 presents examples of where nonprofits have obtained research information for their quick market tests.

Figure 2. Examples of information sources for a quick market test[15]

Type of nonprofit:	Area agency on aging	Girl Scout council	Counseling service
Venture idea	Temporary agency for older part-time workers	Background verification service	Senior personal care service
Product(s)	Provide skilled, experienced older workers to local employers	Reports that verify accuracy of data from job application forms and interviews	Deliver housekeeping and personal care services to at-home elderly
Target customers for the venture	Manufacturing and service businesses needing temporary help to meet fluctuating demands	Labor-intensive employers who face frequent turnover, especially in health care, day care, and security firms	Frail elderly living independently at home, caregivers (especially adult children) of frail elderly
Published sources	Industry reports from National Association of Temporary and Staffing Services; Commerce Department employment reports	Newspaper and business press articles on problems with employee misrepresentation of their backgrounds	U.S. census data; information from a local area agency on aging
Internet sources	U.S. Economic Census; Bureau of Labor Statistics	Web sites of several background search firms	None
Oral sources	Interviews with state officials who work on elder issues; "secret shopper" calls to local temp agencies	Interviews with staff at several local background verification firms; calls to health care and child care nonprofits	Interviews with managers of local elder high rises, internal staff, caregivers of elderly adults, "sandwich generation" staffers

WORKSHEET 4B   Quick Market Test Research Plan

Instructions

❑ Use a separate worksheet for each venture idea.

❑ From Worksheet 4A, draft answers to the questions and then identify gaps and areas requiring more research.

❑ With help from the venture team, other staff, and informal advice from the entrepreneurial committee, use Worksheet 4B to identify how those gaps will get filled.

❑ Do the research, and use the results to complete Worksheets 4A and 4C.

1. What is the venture idea, what is the product or service, and who are the target customers?

   Eldercare services such as housekeeping and personal care services, targeted at older adults and their caregivers.

2. Who will be interviewed and who will conduct each interview?

   The executive director will interview the owner of Seniors First, a similar service located in Omaha. She will also interview a couple of her contacts at the Social Security Administration's data collection department to see if there is some new data available.

   The person in charge of our employee advisory service will talk to a couple of HR directors with whom we work. Suggested questions for each of these interviews will be written by the project leader.

   The counseling services director will identify six clients who match the customer profile for this business, and who, because of their relationship with our organization, might be willing to be interviewed about a service like this.

3. What published sources will be used and who will be responsible for finding them?

   The project leader will gather government reports on seniors and their needs; we receive most of the publications in-house, so the need is to pull them together and summarize them.

4. What Internet sources will be used and who will be responsible for finding them?

   The project leader will review the U.S. Census web site for 2000 census data on the senior population in our metropolitan area. Will also surf business publications from around the country in search of news articles about ventures similar to the one we're considering.

5. How many hours will be put into this, and by what date will the research be completed?

   Target date is June 18. Expect to put in about 20 hours.

Tips for Internet-assisted research

A wealth of useful venture information is available on the Internet. The challenge is to find that information in a timely manner. Here are some suggestions to make your search more focused, efficient, and effective.

Find the key industry or market terms. The words you use to describe your topic may not be the terms typically used in the market or industry you're researching. You might search for "public radio," for example, but find that "noncommercial radio" or "listener-supported radio" appears more often. Once you find a useful site, write down the key words that appear there, and then search again using those terms. One way to find a useful site is to use a directory service such as Yahoo (www.yahoo.com). A related tip: Once you locate a useful site, search for web pages that have links to it. In AltaVista (www.altavist.com), for example, *link:www.neh.fed.us* will locate sites with a link to the National Endowment for the Humanities home page.

Keep track of where you've been. When you find a web site with useful information, print or save the file for later reference, and add a bookmark if you want to return to the site.

The Internet is mostly a free medium. The vast majority of Internet sites are available without a fee, and some fee-based data can be found elsewhere for free. Exceptions you might want to pay for would be a Dun & Bradstreet "business background report" on a potential competitor or a subscription to the online version of *The Wall Street Journal*. You can join various services for a month and then cancel or keep the subscriptions depending on how useful you find them.

Keep a critical perspective. Be sure to evaluate the source as well as the content of any information on the Internet. Data from industry associations, periodicals, and most established companies are generally reliable and up-to-date, while newsgroup postings or Joe's home page may require additional verification. Don't rely on any one piece of information or a single source to make your decisions, unless that source is very credible.

To find something on a large web site, use the site's search engine, if there is one and it's working, or you can use Google's site feature (www.google.com), which often works better. For example, *Maryland site:isquare.com* will locate all the pages within the Small Business Advisor's site that mention the state of Maryland. This won't work for every web site, but it's worth a try.

You'll still need to use the phone and the local library. The Internet should be considered as a supplement, not a substitute, for gathering information. While hundreds of publications can be found online, many more cannot, or are only available in a limited form online. For example, the online version of *The New York Times* offers the current day's edition only, while the CD-ROM version (available at many libraries) includes back issues. The Internet can also be a source for names, addresses, phone numbers, and e-mail addresses of industry experts and potential customers, partners, and suppliers, who can then be contacted to obtain additional information.

Evaluate your ideas; select one for in-depth feasibility analysis

A list of general web sites to use for doing Internet research appears in Appendix C.

After filling in all of the quick market test questions, complete Worksheet 4C: QMT Scorecard on page 204 for each venture idea. A sample is on page 62.

Complete the QMT Twenty Questions and Scorecard worksheets.

WORKSHEET 4C   Quick Market Test Scorecard

Instructions

❑ Use the information from your completed QMT Twenty Questions worksheet (4A) to rate each of your answers.

❑ Use the following ratings to make your evaluation. (A scoring key appears at the end.)

| 5 = yes | 4 = probably | 3 = maybe | 2 = probably not | 1 = no |

Example: **Eldercare Services**

	Rating
Product	
1. Can you clearly describe the product or service?	4
2. Do you know how to produce and deliver it?	4
3. Do you know how customers will find it beneficial to them?	5
Customers	
4. Have you identified your target customers?	5
5. Do you have an existing relationship with these customers?	4
6. Do you have evidence of customer interest?	5
7. Do you know how to sell this product to these customers?	4
8. Are they growing in numbers or buying more each year?	5
9. Do you know what's important to these customers?	4
Advantages	
10. Does this venture build on your core competencies?	4
11. Could you produce and deliver it efficiently?	3
12. Do you know what the competition is for this product?	4
13. Would it be difficult for another firm to replicate your product?	2
14. Is there good reason to expect customers would prefer your product?	4
15. Does this represent a good fit with your mission and key stakeholders?	4
Business Model	
16. Do you have evidence that customers will pay for this and that there is profit potential?	3
17. Could you tolerate, finance, or raise the start-up costs for this venture?	4
18. Do you know the minimum sales level needed to make a profit?	0

(continued)

Worksheet 4C—Quick Market Test Scorecard

	Rating
19. Can you overcome weaknesses your nonprofit will have running this venture?	3
20. Can you find suitable staff (managerial and operational) to operate this venture?	3
Total score	74

SCORING

74+ Impressive! Looks like you're on to something. Proceed to the feasibility study, or, if start-up costs and risks are low, prepare a brief plan, a budget, and *just do it.*

69–73 Gray area. Review the customer and advantage sections carefully before deciding to do a full feasibility study on this idea.

59–68 Probably drop it. Exceptions would be if there are several "0" ratings that, with additional research or revising the concept, might change to higher scores.

< 58 Drop it.

A score of 74 places this venture idea in the "impressive" category, and so this counseling service decided to do a feasibility study.

After scoring each idea, the venture team should discuss the results and decide the fate of each venture idea. Does it warrant further analysis in a feasibility study, is it impractical and should be rejected, or does it need to be modified and retested? If more than one idea passes the QMT, choose the one with the highest score. If none of your ideas pass the test, you will need to modify an idea or go back to the brainstorming drawing board, revisiting your list of brainstormed ideas or brainstorming anew. Although discouraging, it's better for your idea to fail during a quick market test than to fail in the marketplace. Present the worksheets and your conclusions to the entrepreneurial committee and ask for impressions and advice.

Present your results (Worksheets 4A and 4C) first to the venture team and your executive director, and then to the entrepreneurial committee. If the decision is made that the evidence supports proceeding to feasibility market research (Step 5) on one of the venture ideas, solicit the committee's advice and contacts to accomplish this.

In rare cases, it's appropriate to proceed directly to launching a promising venture following the QMT. This makes sense in cases where the start-up costs and risks are minimal, and the nonprofit already has a good understanding of the product and target market. For example, if the venture idea is small in scale and the costs of failure would be minimal, some organizations choose to test the idea by actually starting the venture.

Step 4 summary

You ran the three ideas you chose in Step 3 through a quick market test to pick the one with the greatest chance of succeeding as a venture. You gathered external, market-based data on which to base your decision. The quick market test is a good introduction to and trial run for the kind of in-depth market analysis you will do for the feasibility market research of Step 5. Ideally, you now have one idea—the best of the three you were evaluating—that warrants more research.

Step 5: Do Feasibility Market Research
How to do the research and analysis to obtain market-based data on what it will take to succeed with your venture idea

Time estimate:

Five to ten weeks, 50 to 100 hours of work

Activity summary:

- Develop a feasibility market research plan
- Analyze your customers and competition; identify success factors
- Identify requirements for marketing, operations, pricing, and other factors

By the end of this step, you will have identified the general characteristics your venture needs in order to be profitable. At that point, you will compare those requirements with your organization's capabilities.

Step 5 is where the heavy lifting begins. Starting a business involves significant costs as well as risks; one way to minimize the risks is to understand as much about the venture as possible before you begin. While the quick market test involved a rapid scan to decide which idea was most promising, the feasibility study requires digging much deeper to develop a thorough understanding of a single venture idea. For example, instead of simply identifying the primary competitors, feasibility market research calls for preparing detailed profiles of each of them.

As you spend time researching your venture idea and envisioning how to turn it into a business, you will discover many options to choose from and decisions that must be made for actually running the business. For example, an idea to provide a cultural sensitivity training program to social workers might look at classroom workshops as one option, and online training as another. Or an organization interested in writing a nursing home guide might evaluate self-publishing versus contracting with a publisher, or whether to sell directly to the public or to sell through bookstores.

Keep these options in mind as you fill out the worksheets; use a separate worksheet copy for each major option if the answers will be different. As your research progresses, you may find that some options drop out as impractical or that you can combine options (for example, sell the nursing home guide through both channels). Some organizations find that they need to prepare separate financial analyses (Step 6) to determine which option makes best financial sense.

Here's a basic overview of Step 5. First you will put together a research plan for gathering market-based information about customers, competitors, and success factors.

After conducting the research, you should have a good understanding of each of these areas. Your knowledge in these areas will help you to determine the venture requirements for marketing, operations, pricing, and other factors. Those requirements, in turn, will inform the financial analysis in Step 6.

Parts of feasibility market research

The parts of Step 5 are summarized in the following figure.

Figure 3. Feasibility Market Research Summary

Part	Activities	Time budget
Research plan	Design a feasibility market research plan to do interviews and review documents. Identify: • Customers: contact target customers through one-to-one interviews, surveys, and focus groups • Industry sources: interview industry experts, consultants, and suppliers • Trade associations: review publications and databases; interview officials • Government information and statistics: demographic trends, economic trends • Competitors: find listings in yellow pages and newspapers; review web sites; get annual reports; do secret shopping	6–12 hours
Customers A. Target customers B. Customer interest	Describe target customers and segments; and what their special wants and needs are. Evaluate willingness to pay for your products or services. Assess what it takes to attract them to your venture. Review key referral sources as means of attracting customers.	20–40 hours
Success factors	Summarize what is essential for success with this venture	6–12 hours
Competitors A. Competitor profiles B. Your competitive advantage	Identify key competitors and their strengths and weaknesses. Figure out your competitive strengths and weaknesses for your venture.	10–20 hours
Requirements	From your research identify the requirements for marketing, operations, pricing, and other requirements that must be met to attract target customers.	8–16 hours
Total		**50–100 hours**

Develop a feasibility market research plan

Getting the research done is typically the biggest stumbling block for nonprofit managers. After reading through the information contained in this step, start listing all of the sources that you can think of that might provide answers for the worksheets. If this is a venture idea in an area with which your nonprofit has experience, you and others on staff should be able to come up with a substantial list of sources. Discuss potential sources with your venture team, with senior management, and with the entrepreneurial committee. Organize the suggestions into a market research plan.

Most project leaders find that with help from others in their organization they are able to gather the necessary data. Some organizations feel they will need outside assistance during the market research phase and they contract with a consultant for that purpose. Others have been able to get volunteer student help through a local business school.

Keep in mind that your research plan often evolves as you proceed. Each contact you reach and article you read might suggest useful information sources you won't want to miss. Be sure to keep good notes so you can take advantage of these referrals. The work involves both primary and secondary research techniques. Examples of the former would be interviewing prospective customers, and the latter talking to industry observers and gathering information from the library and the web.

Worksheet 5A: Feasibility Market Research Plan, page 206, includes a list of questions that will help you organize your research. A sample is on page 68.

Project Leader Tasks

- ❑ Write down what you already know for Worksheets 5B through 5F.
- ❑ Prepare an initial draft of your feasibility research plan (Worksheet 5A) to fill in the gaps.
- ❑ Discuss feasibility research plan with venture team. Delegate research duties. Agree on expectations and timetable. Send to entrepreneurial committee for suggestions and contacts.
- ❑ Identify target customers (Worksheet 5B), customer interest (5C), success factors (5D), competitor profiles (5E), and competitive advantage (5F) for this venture.
- ❑ Use these findings to help determine requirements for marketing (5G), operations (5H), pricing (5I), and other requirements (5J) for this venture.
- ❑ Circulate the completed Step 5 worksheets to your venture team. Evaluate whether the requirements represent a good match with your organization's venture audit findings (Step 2). Present to your entrepreneurial committee.

Write down what you already know for Worksheets 5B through 5J. Prepare an initial draft of your feasibility research plan (Worksheet 5A) to fill in the gaps. Discuss feasibility research plan with venture team. Delegate research duties. Agree on expectations and timetable. Send to entrepreneurial committee for suggestions and contacts.

Carry out market research and analysis

Market research and analysis involves gathering extensive data (1) on your target customers and how and why they buy products similar to what you're proposing; (2) on your competitors and what they do to attract customers; and (3) on what it takes to market, produce, and deliver products to these customers.

Every successful business is built on a thorough understanding of its customers and competitors. Business owners often say things like "our customers want this," or "the market is moving in this direction," or "we must do this to stay competitive."

WORKSHEET 5A   Feasibility Market Research Plan

Instructions

❑ Go through the worksheets for Step 5 and fill in what you can.

❑ Note gaps in the worksheets and where verification is needed.

❑ Using this worksheet, develop a research plan to fill in those gaps.

Example: **Nature center gift shop**

1. How will you directly contact target customers to evaluate their interest in and willingness to pay for your products or services? (Examples include informal contact, interviews, surveys, and focus groups.)

    **Mail survey to nature center members. In-person interviews
    of center visitors. Informal focus groups with school and scout
    groups who visit the center.**

2. What knowledgeable people can you contact to get more information about these target customers?

    **We will ask staff and board members for contacts with gift shop
    managers (and other experts in this area) that we can
    interview. We'll review the trip evaluation forms we get
    from school and scout groups.**

3. What trade associations, government agencies, or chambers of commerce will you contact for information about this industry?

    **The Association of Nature Center Administrators regularly conducts
    surveys about the operations, facilities, programs, and services
    of nature centers. As a member of the association we have access to
    information on market studies, membership questions, and surveys
    that the Association has collected. They also do consulting and
    provide technical assistance.**

    **The Museum Store Association, which we will join, has two publica-
    tions that we'll request: (1) *Operations and Financial Information
    Survey Report for Nature Museums*, and (2) *The New Store Workbook: A
    Guide to Remodeling, Expanding and Opening a Museum Store*.**

(continued)

Worksheet 5A—Feasibility Market Research Plan

4. What industry experts, consultants, or suppliers will you contact for information about this industry?

> We'll ask the Museum Store Association to suggest consultants who have expertise in the area of gift shop development. We'll also contact several suppliers of products for nature gift shops, to ask for advice and recommendations.

5. Who else in the industry (preferably noncompetitors) will you contact for information about this industry?

> We'll contact nature center gift shop managers in several other cities. Four that are closest to us in size and number of visitors are: Big Woods Conservation Park, Douglas Science Museum, Great Lakes Interpretive Center, and Mississippi Flyway Center.

6. What kinds of "secret shopping" will you do of competitors to get a feel for their offerings and marketing strategies?

> We will visit gift shops at nearby nature centers, and the local children's museum, science museum, and zoo. We will shop at the Discovery Channel Store, two local bird feeding outlets, and several gardening centers that specialize in native plants. We will also review catalogs and web sites that offer products similar to what we might carry.

7. What kinds of library and Internet research will you undertake to improve your understanding of this industry?

> We will order the last three years of Museum Store, the monthly publication of the Museum Store Association. We will review web sites of other nature centers and of associations dedicated to birding and gardening.

8. What other sources of information will you draw on to help answer the questions in Step 5?

> A recent board member has been involved in the mail-order business for many years, and has agreed to provide us with informal advice for issues that overlap between her business and ours. She also "volunteered" her finance person to advise us on the financial part of the analysis.

Entrepreneurs know that their business survival depends on their customers' decisions. Feasibility market research is done in part so you will know these things *before* deciding to start the venture.

A few definitions will help you with your research. Your *market* consists of all of your target customers. It's often useful to subdivide your market into *customer segments* that share similar characteristics and buying habits. For example, the market for the nature center gift shop can be divided into the nature enthusiasts segment and the school/scout groups segment. Sometimes the term *market segment* is used instead of customer segment; they mean the same thing.

> Your *market* consists of all of your target customers. *Customer segments* share similar characteristics and buying habits.

There is often a certain amount of overlap between customer segments. For the nature center gift shop, some children may belong to both the school/scout segment (via weekday field trips) and to the casual nature enthusiasts segment (via weekend trips with family). That's not a problem. First of all, some overlap between segments makes sense if each segment brings in new target customers; in this case, it was estimated that only 20 percent of the nature enthusiasts were families with children under eighteen. (See sample Worksheet 5B.) Secondly, even when two different segments include some of the same people—say the children in this case—the segments indicate differences in how customers are likely to interact with the gift shop, and thus what kind of marketing strategies will work with them. It has been observed that children in school groups shop differently and pay attention to different things compared to when they visit with their parents or grandparents.

Analyze your customers

During your customer analysis work you will

- Define and characterize target customers
- Measure customer interest

Incidentally, if you're looking into more than one option, you may need to fill out separate worksheets for each option, depending on the nature of the differences. This would be especially true if the options involve different groups of customers.

A. Define target customers

Customer research begins with a clear description of the people you will be trying to attract as customers—your target customers. In the quick market test you probably used a general description. Now you need to be more specific.

Who are they? What do you already know about them? What is the geographic area from which most of them will come? How old are they? What percentage are male, what percentage female? If target customers are companies rather than individuals, similar questions need to be addressed. What kinds of companies? Geographic area? Sizes? Industry? Who makes the purchasing decisions at these companies?

Now, given what you already know about these customers, how do they naturally split into customer segments? Be specific. As mentioned, a segment represents a group of customers who have similar perspectives and needs relative to your product. For example, a nonprofit interested in coordinating conferences realized that teachers have different needs and expectations for conferences than health care professionals. Finally, indicate whether demand in each market segment is growing, stable, or declining.

As you do your research keep in mind the "80/20 Rule." For most businesses, roughly 80 percent of sales come from 20 percent of their customers. Rather than researching every possible customer, focus your efforts on the customer segments that are most likely to reflect the most sales.

Worksheet 5B: Target Customers[16] on page 208 describes how to clarify who your customers are. A sample is on page 72. Review the questions and sample answers provided, noting the level of detail.

Identify target customers for this venture.

B. Measure customer interest

The second and usually the most difficult part of customer research is to measure the level of customer interest in the proposed product or service. Do *customers* want these things? How much interest is there? What are they willing to pay? Since you will be estimating sales for these customers, measuring customer interest is a vital part of your feasibility work. This research may also offer insights into operational and marketing needs, which will help you complete the worksheets on requirements.

The best way to find out if customers are interested in your venture idea is to ask them. If your nonprofit already works with these customers, use your organization's relationship with them to find out their interest. This is where a survey can be very effective. Information from a survey can be supplemented with data that your organization collects about its current constituents on a regular basis. For example, a counseling agency contemplating a new service can track how many calls it already gets for that service, calls that it previously referred to another organization.

A variety of techniques can be used to test your concept with customers:

- A *survey* could be distributed to ascertain customer appeal.
- *Focus groups* could be convened to assess customer needs, preferences, and reactions.[17]
- A pilot for a service or a prototype for a product could be created and offered to a sample group of customers to get their reactions and level of interest.

WORKSHEET 5B   Target Customers

Instructions

❑ Fill in what you already know about your target customers. Identify where the gaps are and where additional verification is needed.

❑ Note the gaps as you develop and carry out your feasibility research plan (Worksheet 5A).

❑ Return to this worksheet and fill in the gaps.

Example: **Nature center gift shop**

1. Who are the target customers for this venture? Be specific. *Profile* them. What's the *size* of each segment? What's the growth *trend* in this segment: fast growing, slow growing, stable, or declining? (Fast-growing segments increase by at least 10 percent per year.) What *benefits* do these customers perceive from this venture?

Customer segment		Description
Nature enthusiasts (includes our members)	Profile:	Emotional tie to nature, enjoy native birds and wildflowers. Typically 40-65 in age, suburban, middle income. Often tend nature gardens and bird feeders at home. About 20% are families with children under 18. About 5% are tourists (live 100+ miles away).
	Size:	Of our 120,000 annual visitors, about 20,000 are in this segment. Center currently has 1,200 members ($25 individual, $38 family), who visit the center an average of three times per year.
	Trend:	Growing
	Benefits:	Information and items to enhance their experience with nature.
Casual nature strollers	Profile:	Enjoy nature (and nature centers) as just another outdoor activity. Typically somewhat younger (25-50) than nature enthusiasts, also middle income and suburban. About 50% are families with children under 18.
	Size:	Account for about 40,000 of our visitors.
	Trend:	Stable
	Benefits:	Impulsive gift buying if something catches their attention.

(continued)

Worksheet 5B—Target Customers

Customer segment	Description
School and scout groups	Profile: Outdoor, educational activity organized by teachers or scout leaders. Grades 4-9. 50% suburban, 40% urban, 10% rural. Size: About 60,000 children visit the center each year as part of a school or scout group. Trend: Fast growth Benefits: Teachers/scout leaders: supports educational objectives. Children: enjoy being outdoors, collecting stuffed animals, toys, and plastic bugs.

2. What products would interest these customers?

The shop will offer retail items with a nature or science theme for adults and children in a number of categories, including books, clothing, posters, CDs and videos, gifts, equipment for outdoor pursuits such as hiking, birding and gardening, and stuffed animals, toys, and educational materials. The shop will also specialize in birding supplies and prairie/native plants gardening to complement the center's expertise. Near the shop will be an area with tables and chairs that offers light refreshments for sale such as soda, spring water, pastries, and ice cream.

3. How do customers typically get information about these types of products? Are there intermediaries through whom this kind of a venture tends to attract customers?

People visit nature centers to view nature, learn about natural science, participate in programs, and visit the exhibits. By and large, shopping at the gift shop is spontaneous rather than planned. If the store's appearance appeals to them and they are interested in shopping, they will stop in and shop. Thus, the nature center itself is the primary intermediary, by, in effect, endorsing the gift shop and referring visitors to it. For that reason, successful efforts by the nature center to attract visitors will also benefit the gift shop.

A secondary set of referral sources would be local media stories about the center, listings in local publications, the tourist information office, and nature center guidebooks.

Some data on customer interest can be obtained by talking with industry experts and observers, but such discussions should supplement—not replace—testing your concept with actual customers. The easiest and most frequently used technique is simply to interview prospective customers.

Here are several examples of how nonprofits have obtained research data from their prospective customers:

Product/service	Customer testing strategy
Continuing education courses specifically for social workers	Phone surveys of social workers who have attended previous training sessions
Child care referral database service	Interviews set up with local human resources directors of large employers
Catering service	Pilot offered to a few customers during the holiday season
Gift catalog	Two-page mini-catalog mailed to a sample of nonprofit's mailing list

Along with assessing customer interest, you will need to estimate the amount of sales that interest might generate. There are essentially three ways to do this:

- *Logical expansion of current sales.* If your organization already provides products to these customers, you may be able to estimate how sales would increase if certain changes or improvements were made, based on prior sales experience and observations of the marketplace.

- *"Borrow" a model from elsewhere.* Somewhere an organization is operating a venture similar to the one you're looking into. If you can find the organization, its staff will probably share their experiences with you, as long as they don't see you as a competitor. (As noted previously, many nonprofit ventures will share information *even if* you might compete with them.) You can use their experience (and numbers, if available) to estimate customer interest for your venture, adjusting to fit local circumstances. For example, a nonprofit working in a low-income neighborhood in Baltimore was interested in creating a venture to recondition discarded refrigerators and resell them cheaply to local residents.[18] To help estimate customer interest, it compared notes with a nonprofit operating a similar business on the West Coast. Internet searches, journal articles, conference networking, and word-of-mouth can help you find comparable ventures.

- *Apply industry statistics.* An association exists for just about every imaginable venture. These associations collect data from their members on a variety of topics that can help you estimate potential sales, as well as shed light on a number of other market research questions. For a relatively small fee they often sell reports that summarize this information. For example, the Museum Store Association collects extensive sales data for museum shops. Such information is useful for museums contemplating creation or expansion of their gift shops.

Next, identify the key *trends* that support or detract from selling to your target customers. This is where you describe changes in the world that will help (or hinder) your efforts. For example, a trend that concerns many public radio stations is that the audience for classical music is getting older every year. Similarly, many social service nonprofits carefully monitor major social trends to be sure their services remain on track.

Worksheet 5C: Customer Interest on page 210 will help you evaluate customer interest. A sample is on page 76. Note the level of detail in the sample answers.

Evaluate customer interest in this venture.

Are your customers different from your end users?

Feasibility studies look primarily at *customers* rather than *end users*. A customer is the person who decides to buy the product, which is not always the same as the person who uses or pays for it. Suppose a nonprofit seeks to develop adaptive software so young children with physical disabilities can use computers. While children are the end users, parents and educators are the customers, since they decide what to purchase. Another example would be a training program directed at nurses. The nurses are the customers if they decide where they will get their training, even if their employers actually pay for it. Be sure you are considering customers when you conduct your feasibility study.

WORKSHEET 5C   Customer Interest

Instructions

❑ Fill in what you already know and what you still need to find out.
  Identify where your information gaps are.

❑ Use the information you gather while doing market research (Worksheet 5A)
  to complete your answers to these questions.

Example: **Nature center gift shop**

1. Detail the evidence demonstrating that your target customers will be interested in purchasing these products. Who else is selling related products that suggests this could be successful?

   We've successfully sold food, books, t-shirts, seed packets, and bird feeding supplies during our spring and fall migration celebrations. We surveyed our members, volunteers and mailing list: 78% rated opening a gift shop as "favorable" and 64% said they would or probably would shop there. Those surveyed expressed a preference for a range of products - including guide books, posters, native seeds, gifts, and binoculars.

   We interviewed our visitors: 63% said the following statement was "true" or "mostly true" - "I wish there was something I could take home to remember this visit," and 33% said they would or probably would consider purchasing something if there was a gift shop at the center. About the same percentage expressed an interest in having more refreshments available (currently we have two vending machines). A casual survey of exercisers and playground users showed a favorable impression of having snacks and refreshments available.

   To gauge interest in specific product categories, survey responders were asked to check off those items they would be interested in purchasing at the gift shop.

   We also gathered comparative data from other nature centers. Gift shop data from four nature centers closest to ours in size and attendance are as follows:

(continued)

Worksheet 5C—Customer Interest

Name	Nature center visitors	Store size (sq. ft.)	Sales	Sales/ visitor	Sales/square feet
Big Woods Conservation Park	90,000	700	$135,000	$1.50	$193
Douglas Science Museum	130,000	650	$205,000	$1.58	$315
Great Lakes Interpretive Center	80,000	750	$175,000	$2.19	$233
Mississippi Flyway Center	120,000	600	$160,000	$1.33	$267
Averages	—	—	—	$1.65	$252

2. What trends in the marketplace provide further evidence that you will be able to sell these products to these customers?

   An increasing number of nature centers have gift shops. Some organizations have created mail-order catalogs to sell products. Most of these activities are reported to positively impact their finances.

   Plant nurseries specializing in native plants and stores devoted to bird feeding and birding have opened in our area recently. The shelf space devoted to these topics at local bookstores increases each year. The library has noted greater interest in these topics also.

3. Finally, what does your research into customer interest tell you about the likely quantity of annual customers and sales for each of the customer segments? Consider what this might be after the venture is "fully established," which is typically after two or three years of operation.

   Given our 120,000 annual visitors, and conservatively estimating average sales of $1.50 per visitor (see Question #1, above), potential sales would be about $180,000 per year. We anticipate that half would come from the school and scout group segment, with 25% from nature enthusiasts and 25% from casual nature strollers.

Identify success factors

Success factors describe what will be essential to succeed with this venture. They represent a short list of the things that the venture has to do well to attract and retain customers. They aren't the same for every venture, and they often change over time. From your organization's experience, you may already know what some of these success factors are. In most cases, you will need to do more market research to sharpen your list of success factors.[19]

Be sure to consider a variety of types of success factors. Most success factors concern customers in some fashion (what features and benefits will be essential to satisfy their expectations), but others focus primarily on operations (qualifications of staff, ability to produce at a certain defined quality level, specialized equipment) or marketing (name recognition, access to customers).

Here's an example. A nonprofit wanted to produce and sell an independent guide to metro nursing homes. Management interviewed a sample of their target customers—the middle-aged children of functionally declining seniors. They also reviewed related products available in their town and elsewhere. Finally, they met with publishing experts. They decided on the following success factors:

- Compelling cover art
- Up-to-date nursing home data
- Easy-to-use presentation of content
- Suitable endorsements
- Distribution agreements with local bookstore chains

You'll note that in the example above, the success factors are general in nature. They should be general at this point. Later, during the requirements section of your feasibility work, you will specify what actually must be done to fulfill each success factor. For instance, "up-to-date nursing home data" would be further defined as to how current such information needs to be.

Worksheet 5D: Success Factors on page 211 helps you identify what your venture needs to be feasible. A sample follows. Again note the level of detail in the example.

Identify success factors for this venture.

WORKSHEET 5D   Success Factors

Instructions

❑ Fill in what you already know and what you still need to find out. Identify
the gaps in the information.

❑ Don't worry if you're not sure in which category a given success factor belongs;
pick the one it fits in best.

❑ Use the information you gathered while doing market research (Worksheet 5A)
to complete your answers to these questions.

Example: **Nature center gift shop**

1. What are the *customer* success factors for this venture idea?

Customer success factor	Why does this matter to customers?
Products that appeal to target customers	Retail customers can be finicky and dynamic with their buying preferences. They have many choices about where and what to buy. Keeping up on the latest trends will be important to keep our inventory fresh.
Presentation that appeals to target customers	How products are presented makes a huge difference in buying decisions. Gift shop purchases are often impulse buys and an attractive presentation can make the sale.
Wide price mix with at least 50% under $10	Pricing at least half of the items below $10 entices more customers to buy, and is also important to maintain a quick rate of inventory turnover.
Friendly sales staff with extensive product knowledge	Customers like to feel cared for and want to have confidence in the salesperson helping them.

(continued)

2. What are the *marketing* success factors for this venture idea?

Marketing success factor	Why is this essential for success with this venture?
High visibility among target customers	The key is turning visitors into gift shop browsers, and then into customers. A convenient, well-signed location where all visitors to the nature center will naturally walk by the shop increases the chances they will enter it.
Deliver frequent reminders to target customers	We need to keep reminding visitors about the store, and that we have items for sale that will enhance their enjoyment of nature or would make great gifts.

3. What are the *operational* success factors for this venture idea?

Operational success factor	Why is this essential for success with this venture?
Cost efficiencies and control	Careful control of display, marketing and staff costs is essential to maintain profitability.

Analyze your competition

There are two parts to understanding competition. First, you must understand who and what you are competing with. Then you must identify your unique competitive advantage—the reasons why customers will choose you over the competition. In other words, who are your competitors, and what is it about your venture and its products that customers will perceive as superior?

A. Profile primary competitors

The first part of this task is to identify and profile competitors. What do your target customers see as key alternatives to your product or service? Think broadly about customer choices and competitors to make sure you don't miss any important ones. Typically there are four sources of competition:

1. Organizations that offer similar services that provide the customer with a similar experience. Such organizations are usually obvious and easy to list. For example, a day care provider competes with other day care providers and an art museum competes with other art museums.

2. Organizations that offer the same product in a different way or at a different price. Door-to-door candy sales also compete with grocery stores, convenience marts, and direct-mail catalogs.

3. Organizations that compete for the same customers but with different offerings. For example, arts organizations with very different performances often compete for the same arts-oriented audience. Or a community center that wants to start up a new yoga class has competition even if the yoga class will be the only one in town; there may be an aerobics class that represents an alternative for some of the center's target customers.

4. Other options competing for customer attention, money, or time. For example, some customers choose to do without a useful service altogether, even if it's free. They may be too busy, too tired, or just not feel like getting out of the house if they don't have to. They may choose to watch television rather than attend a health club.

Worksheet 5E: Competitor Profiles on page 213 helps you list your competition for each market segment and develop brief descriptions of each competitor. A sample is on page 82. Note the level of detail.

Profile the competitors this venture will face.

WORKSHEET 5E   Competitor Profiles

Instructions

❑ Fill in what you already know. Identify what you still need to find out for this worksheet.

❑ Use the information you gathered while carrying out your feasibility market research plan (Worksheet 5A) to complete your answers to these questions.

❑ Questions about competitor pricing strategies appear in Worksheet 5I.

Example: `Nature center gift shop`

1. Who are the most likely competitors for your business and its target customers? Consider all types of competition as described on page 81 under the heading "Profile primary competitors." Indicate how the competition may be different for each of your customer segments.

Customer segment	Similar product and experience	Similar product, different experience	Same customers, different offerings	Other alternatives
Segment 1 Nature enthusiasts	Riverview Nature Center gift shop	Gardening stores; birding/bird seed stores	LL Bean catalog; public TV	Surf web
Segment 2 Casual nature strollers	Riverview Nature Center gift shop	History center gift shop; catalog and web sites	Art museum gift shop; shopping at the mall	Do without
Segment 3 School and scout groups	Gift shops at science museum and aquarium	Discovery Channel stores	Children's Theater; sports activities; web research and programs	Invite naturalist to class-room

(continued)

2. Which of these do you consider to be your primary competitors? Why? (Pick at least three competitors who present the closest similarity with your venture, first in terms of customers—the alternative they would most likely choose if your venture ceased to exist—and second in terms of products or services. Explain why each one was picked.)

> <u>Riverview Nature Center.</u> High overlap in visitors (in our surveys, RNC is the most frequent response to the question "what other nature centers have you visited in the past 12 months?"), and likely to be the most similar in products as well.

> <u>Discovery Channel stores.</u> Clearly the best example in the metro area of effective marketing of nature and science-related products to families with children under 18.

> <u>Birds of a Feather.</u> Best example of a specialty store selling birding and bird feeding supplies in the metro area.

3. Construct a brief profile of *each* of your primary competitors, including customers, size, products or services, and areas of strength or special appeal.

> The Riverview Nature Center gift shop is relatively small (about 400 square feet), appears to serve roughly the same customer segments that we would serve, and offers a similar inventory but with more emphasis on riparian habitat materials. With approximately 60,000 annual visitors to the center, we understand the gift shop does about $80,000 in annual sales.

> The Discovery Channel stores are colorful, brightly lit spaces in major malls designed primarily to appeal to children with an unusual assortment of educational toys. The store we visited had about 850 square feet, and we were unable to estimate annual sales.

> Birds of a Feather, located in a suburban strip mall with about 600 square feet, emphasizes "upscale" birding and bird feeding supplies. Its customers appear to be closest to our nature enthusiasts segment.

4. Describe the communication strategies that each primary competitor uses for its marketing efforts.

> The Riverview Nature Center gift shop relies primarily on visitor traffic for its customer base and promotes itself with product displays and signage, in the member newsletter, in program information, and on the center's web site. They also occasionally buy

(continued)

small newspaper ads for specials during high visitation periods (fall and spring migration).

The Discovery Channel stores are located in major malls. They promote themselves to thousands of walk-by shoppers daily with attractive signage and appealing window displays. They are affiliated with the cable TV Discovery Channel which gives them good name recognition with adults and children alike. They also buy large newspaper ads on a regular basis.

Birds of a Feather mails out a quarterly newsletter with advertised specials and takes out small ads in the city and neighborhood newspapers. They have a Frequent Birders Club that rewards repeat customers with points that can be converted into discounts or free merchandise. They have a large sign and window display at their location in a strip mall.

B. Identify your competitive advantage

The second part of analyzing the competition is identifying your unique *competitive advantages*—the reasons why customers will choose your product or service over the competition. You need to objectively compare your proposed venture with its primary competitors to determine why customers would prefer your product. To do this, you rate each of your competitors according to the success factors you've determined for the business. Often the hardest part of this analysis is being objective about your own venture. Usually the best way to make sure you remain objective is to assume the new venture will share the same general characteristics as your nonprofit, at least initially. It's usually best not simply to assume weaknesses will disappear or a new person will be hired who can overcome the nonprofit's problems.[20]

Worksheet 5F: Competitive Advantage[21] on page 215 helps you rate your proposed venture alongside your competition. The worksheet calls for you to place all your success factors on the vertical axis and the competing businesses, including yours, on the horizontal axis. You then rate each one on a scale of 1 to 5. In most cases, your organization will not be the high scorer for each success factor; in the sample worksheet that follows, the nonprofit ranked itself as the high scorer in only one of the success factors. Its overall scores, however, indicate that it has a good competitive advantage in the marketplace.

Figure out your competitive advantage with this venture.

WORKSHEET 5F   Competitive Advantage

Instructions

❑ Pull out your answers to Worksheets 5D (Success Factors) and 5E (Competitor Profiles). Place them on a grid with your business and the competition across the top and success factors along the side.

❑ Using this information, and what you know about your organization and its capabilities, complete the remainder of the worksheet.

Example: **Nature center gift shop**

1. From Worksheet 5D, what are the success factors for this venture idea?

   - **Products that appeal to target customers**
   - **Presentation that appeals to target customers**
   - **Wide price mix with at least 50% under $10**
   - **Friendly sales staff with extensive product knowledge**
   - **High visibility among target customers**
   - **Deliver frequent reminders to target customers**
   - **Cost efficiencies and control**

2. From Worksheet 5E, who will your key competitors be?

   - **Riverview Nature Center gift shop**
   - **Discovery Channel stores**
   - **Birds of a Feather**

3. On each of the success factors, how will you compare with these competitors? It is important to be objective and realistic rather than promotional. With rare exceptions, only one organization can be ranked with a "5" as the market leader for any success factor. If you find that your answers will differ markedly by customer segment, create a separate table for each segment.

   See table on next page.

(continued)

Competitive Advantage Table

Segment: **Casual Nature Strollers**

Competitor: 5 = major strength   4 = strength 3 = neutral   2 = weakness   1 = major weakness

Success Factor:	Us	Riverview Nature Center	Discovery Channel Stores	Birds of a Feather	Catalog/ Web Sites
Products that appeal to target customers	4	4	5	4	3
Presentation that appeals to target customers	4	3	3	5	2
Wide price mix with at least 50% under $10	3	3	2	3	5
Friendly sales staff with extensive product knowledge	4	3	5	3	1
High visibility among target customers	5	3	4	4	3
Deliver frequent reminders to target customers	4	3	3	4	2
Cost efficiencies and control	3	3	3	4	4
Total score	27	22	25	27	20

4. What does this table (and other data you have gathered) indicate about the relative strengths of your key competitors?

> The Discovery Channel stores and Birds of a Feather appear
> to be our closest competitors. Discovery's strengths are
> in name recognition, advertising (they can afford a big ad

(continued)

budget), buying capabilities (their sheer size and multiple locations allow them to spot trends quicker than we can), presentation (they can afford expensive layouts), and cost efficiencies and control (with multiple stores they can purchase items at lower cost than we can).

An advantage that Birds of a Feather will have over us is their convenient location, the customer base they've built over the ten years they've been in business, and their specialization in birds.

While the Riverview Nature Center appears somewhat lower on this chart, they will still be a significant competitor. They have the advantage of having started their store five years earlier; on the other hand, we can learn by imitating their successes and avoiding their mistakes.

Finally, catalogs and web sites are something to keep aware of but are not currently seen as primary competition. Gift shop customers generally like to touch and feel products before purchasing.

5. What are *your* competitive advantages?

We expect the gift shop to benefit substantially from its physical location as part of the nature center. Visitors are clearly a "captive market," in the sense that we have an opportunity to attract them to the store while they are here feeling good about their visit to the center. At that moment, our competitors are far away, both physically and in the minds of our visitors. This is true for school groups as well as adults.

And while we expect to be the market leader in only one of the success factors, at least initially, doing well on each of them will increase our chances for success with these customers.

6. What are your competitive disadvantages?

One disadvantage is our location, which, while within the metro area, is not as convenient as stores located in local malls. This may work to our disadvantage during the heavy shopping season from mid-November to the end of December. A second disadvantage is that we won't be stocking some items that may sell well but don't fit with the center.

Identify requirements

The next major task is to translate your research into requirements to operate this venture. Essentially this involves converting the success factors from Worksheet 5D into specific requirements; you may also find requirements beyond the success factors. There are four parts to the requirements task:

- Marketing
- Operations
- Pricing
- Other requirements and approvals

Establishing these requirements, and later estimating the costs to meet them, will help you evaluate the feasibility of this venture idea. Moreover, if your feasibility study comes out positive and the decision is made to prepare a business plan to start the venture, these requirements will prove helpful when you write the marketing and operational plan portions of the business plan.

Requirements are essentially lists of what any organization opening a business like this needs to accomplish in marketing, operations, and pricing. On the other hand, a business plan describes precisely the actions *your venture* will take to satisfy the requirements.

Here's an example to clarify the difference between requirements and a business plan. Suppose a venture idea called for opening a thrift shop. Research from talking with thrift shops in other cities and analyzing market conditions and competitors in your community suggests several requirements. It should be located within a particular geographical area (matching the economic profile of successful thrift shops in other cities), and sited on a particular kind of location (busy thoroughfare, sufficient off-street parking, adjacent businesses that attract similar customers), with a certain minimum square footage and a loading dock. In contrast, the operational plan, as part of the business plan, contains decisions on precisely *where* the thrift shop will be located, *why* the location meets these operational requirements, and *how* the space will be set up, furnished, and stocked.

A. Marketing requirements

Marketing requirements is where you figure out what it will take to attract paying customers to your business. There is no magic to this. Successful marketing does not require a marketing genius. What it does require is to study your customers' preferences and choices and then to find ways to adapt and present your offerings to satisfy *their* preferences and to identify methods to communicate how your offerings benefit *them*.

Marketing can be divided into two categories, *research* and *communications*. While there is often a tendency to jump right into designing communications such as brochures, direct mail, or advertisements, it works best to use research to figure out what kinds of communications will be most effective. Assuming that you've done the research to complete the earlier worksheets in this step, you already have marketing research data that can be used for this purpose.

Review whom you identified as your target customers (Worksheet 5B), why they will be interested in your offerings (5C), what the key factors are for succeeding with this business (5D), what kinds of competition you can expect (5E), and how your venture would likely stack up against the competitors (5F). This information will help you figure out the marketing requirements for this venture idea.

Identifying marketing requirements is generally straightforward once you have this information in place. And, if you decide to write a business plan for this idea, the marketing requirements worksheet will help you write a marketing plan for the venture.[22]

Often the best source for ideas on marketing requirements comes from reviewing the marketing strategies used by your key competitors and others in this industry, such as similar ventures operating in different geographic areas. They've probably been working on the same marketing issues you will be facing, and studying their efforts can help inform yours. If necessary, dig to find out more about how they communicate with their customers. Industry associations and trade groups can also offer valuable perspective on this topic.

Worksheet 5G: Marketing Requirements on page 218 helps you convert your research on success factors, customer interests, and competition into marketing requirements. A sample is on page 90.

Identify marketing requirements for this venture.

WORKSHEET 5G   Marketing Requirements

Instructions

❑ Using Target Customers (Worksheet 5B), Customer Interest (5C), Success Factors (5D), and Competitor Profiles (5E), and with help from other members of your venture team, answer the following questions.

❑ If you have difficulty answering the questions, you may need to do more market research.

Example: **Nature center gift shop**

1. What did you identify in Worksheet 5D as the key customer and marketing success factors for this venture idea?

   - **Products that appeal to target customers**
   - **Presentation that appeals to target customers**
   - **Wide price mix with at least 50% under $10**
   - **Friendly sales staff with extensive product knowledge**
   - **High visibility among target customers**
   - **Deliver frequent reminders to target customers**

2. What did you identify about customer interests in Worksheets 5B and 5C that might suggest marketing requirements for this venture idea? Separate by customer segments if appropriate.

   Nature enthusiasts: communications must support notion that gift shop fits in nicely with the values of the nature center. Emphasize items with a practical or educational component. Remind them that their purchases help support and sustain the center. Consider placing ads in local birding and gardening newsletters.

   Nature strollers: remind them of convenience of buying gifts while they're visiting the center — no extra trip required. Especially during prime gift-giving times (December holidays, Valentine's Day, etc.). For ads or press releases, mention something that's available for free (say, a roadside wildflower key) that can be picked up at the gift shop, as an enticement to get them into the store.

   School and scout groups: Younger children like to touch and play with objects before purchasing them. Engage their interest by placing inexpensive, durable items within their reach. Put up posters of prairie flowers and animals. Create prepackaged $2 and $5 gift boxes for school and scout groups to purchase and distribute to the children on the trip. Use recycled and recyclable materials as much as possible. Displays should include bright, cheery colors.

(continued)

Worksheet 5G—Marketing Requirements

3. What communication strategies of competitors did you identify in question 4 of Worksheet 5E?

> **Riverview Nature Center**: communications effort mostly focused on visitors to the center, with signage and product displays. Occasional newspaper ads.

> **Discovery Channel stores**: large ads in major papers; promos on the Discovery Channel. Frequent Shoppers Club; location in major malls; attractive displays.

> **Birds of a Feather**: small ads in neighborhood newspapers, quarterly newsletter to its mailing list. Frequent Birders Club. Large sign and window display.

4. As identified in your research, what communication strategies are used by similar but non-competing firms—for example, businesses in another city, or businesses that target the same customer segments but with different products?

> **The gift shop at Mississippi Flyway Center finds that its best marketing effort is to focus on its visitors rather than the public at large. To do that, they moved the shop from the back of the building to a space near the entrance, and prominently display replicas of popular or special exhibits just outside the shop. They've also worked with the park cafeteria to place ads on the back of each sales receipt offering a $2 discount for any purchase above $15. The entrance ticket itself offers a similar discount.**

> **They also pointed out the importance of getting and maintaining accurate listings in published directories and various free listings including web sites.**

5. Now, review your list of competitors (Worksheet 5E, question 1). There were probably several that you did *not* describe as primary competitors (Worksheet 5E, question 2). Considering those secondary competitors (whom your customers will sometimes perceive as their alternatives), are there marketing requirements to increase the odds that customers will come to you rather than pursue these alternatives?

> **The largest issue here concerns the Internet, which we believe reflects secondary competition for two of our segments: nature enthusiasts and school/scout groups. We believe it is now or will soon be a requirement to have an online component to any gift shop that serves these two segments.**

(continued)

Also, another secondary form of competition is the gift shops at the art museum and the children's theater. Both stores appear very successful. A requirement for any gift shop would be to occasionally "secret shop" these stores to observe their product selection and presentation, to see what approaches might be transferable.

6. What advice about marketing requirements have you obtained from industry experts, trade associations, or consultants working in this area?

A couple of suggestions from the Museum Store Association:

- Establish a name, logo, and visual theme for the store, and consistently use them in signage and all materials that relate to the store (brochures, shopping bags, web site, etc.).

- Utilize repetition of messages about the store in as many marketing vehicles as possible, including mention of the store in every piece of literature produced by the nature center.

7. Finally, how would you translate the above information into a set of marketing requirements for this venture idea? Include requirements for ongoing marketing *research* (e.g., customer surveys, competitor analysis) as well as for communication *strategies* (such as promotional efforts).

We organized the marketing requirements into three categories: product selection, presentation, and communication. Facility issues are discussed under operational requirements.

Product selection

- Products must fit with the values of the nature center, but must also appeal to our customers and sell quickly.
- Products must appeal to children. Store manager will need to keep current on changing tastes, from dinosaurs one year to astronauts the next.
- Weekly tracking of sales by product to highlight and reorder fast-selling merchandise, and remove slow-moving stock.

Presentation

- Attractive, highly visible signage that pulls park visitors into the gift shop. Placement of attractive items at gift shop entrance that catch the attention of each customer segment.

(continued)

Worksheet 5G—Marketing Requirements

- Placement of toy bins at young kid level (i.e., 18 inches above the floor) near the shop entrance to attract children and provide them the opportunity to "touch and feel" objects before purchasing them.
- Style uniformity for all signage and print materials, so they are consistent in font, color, logo use, and so on. Examples include brochures, shopping bags, and web site.

<u>Communication</u>

- Mechanism in place to do frequent surveys of visitors and customers to identify their interests and impressions.
- Coordinate with nature center staff to leverage communication efforts. For example, starting and ending naturalist tours at the gift shop, holding special events in the store (such as lectures, readings, how-to demonstrations), and mentioning the gift shop in brochures, newsletters, and press releases.
- Reminders that all purchases help support the nature center.
- Collect customer names, addresses, and purchases for gift shop's database. Regular mailings about special events in the store (such as readings or how-to demonstrations) and sales.

B. Operational requirements

What must be done to produce and deliver products or services? Through market research and interviewing industry experts, you should have a good handle on what it takes to run this venture. Now you must translate that information into a list of the *operational requirements* necessary to make the venture work.

In most businesses, operational requirements can be divided into six categories: facility, equipment, production processes, supply chain, staffing, and key ratios. Disruption in any one of these areas will create problems for the venture—that's why they are operational requirements. Since the venture you are considering is grounded in your core competencies, you usually already have some of these operational requirements in place.

1. *Facility:* The type of facility required for the venture to succeed. For example, a program that coordinates many outside contractors may need only a single small office, while a program to rehab and sell used appliances may require a warehouse with a loading dock and a storefront.

2. *Equipment:* The kinds of equipment needed to run the venture. The equipment may range from a toll-free telephone line and credit-card charging system to sophisticated machinery and delivery vehicles.

3. *Production processes:* The processes necessary to deliver the products or services promised by the venture. For example, a publishing venture may require editorial services, graphic design, and printing, while an in-home care program may require detailed supervisory and case management protocol.

4. *Supply chain:* The vendor relationships required for the venture. A venture requiring contract health aides, for example, may need to build a long-term relationship with a broker for such services. An on-street arts program may require relationships with contract performers and artists. A home rehab business will need relationships with building suppliers.

5. *Staffing:* The type and level of staffing required. In some cases, no new staff are needed, but time is shifted from existing duties. In other ventures, additional management, professional, and support staff may all be required.

6. *Key ratios:* The ratios that your market research has determined are standard requirements for the industry that you are entering. The venture manager will track and manage these ratios, because they will largely determine the venture's success. All ventures track sales, operating expenses (especially as a percent of sales), and profits, but there are usually several additional ratios for each venture idea. For example, a venture that provides training might include ratios such as average workshop size (need twelve participants to break even, twenty to meet profit goals), operating expenses as a percent of sales, and so on. Sometimes the ratios are numbers the venture has little direct control over, but which can have a dramatic impact on the business; in the case of a nature center gift shop, the number of nature center visitors is an example of this.

Worksheet 5H: Operational Requirements on page 221 helps you define the venture's operational requirements for each of the six categories. A sample follows.

Identify the operational requirements for this venture.

WORKSHEET 5H   Operational Requirements

Instructions

❑ With help from other members of your venture team, answer the following questions. Use Worksheet 5D: Success Factors and Worksheet 5E: Competitor Profiles for details.

❑ It's not uncommon to have difficulty answering some of the questions. This indicates a need for more market research. If your research is adequate, the worksheet should go quickly.

Example: **Nature center gift shop**

1. What did you identify in Worksheet 5D as the key operational success factors for this venture idea? Also list any customer and marketing success factors that have an operational component to them (they usually do).

   - **Cost efficiencies and control**
   - **Products that appeal to target customers**
   - **Presentation that appeals to target customers**
   - **Wide price mix with at least 50% under $10**
   - **Friendly sales staff with extensive product knowledge**
   - **High visibility among target customers**
   - **Deliver frequent reminders to target customers**

2. Facility: What type of facility will be needed to satisfy the success factors? If you expect to use space the nonprofit currently has control over, what improvements will be needed? If new space will be needed, what are the requirements for that space?

   Discussions with other nature center gift shop managers indicate that we'll need at least 600 square feet of sales space, located near the front of the visitor center that allows for admission-free access to the store.

   Adjacent to the shop there should be a friendly, outdoor space for visitors to congregate, enjoy refreshments, and wait for naturalist tours to begin. There should be a window display overlooking the entrance sidewalk that showcases colorful items that catch the attention of pedestrians, especially children.

   Fixtures and floor plan need to be architecturally consistent with the rest of the building. Suitable bookshelves and display tables need to be constructed and installed. Displays need to feature dynamic themes that have high visual impact.

(continued)

> The shop needs to have a look and feel comparable to that of the cen-
> ter itself; visitors need to feel that they have not left the center as
> they enter the gift shop.

3. Equipment: What kinds of equipment will be needed to run this venture and to meet the success factors?

> Point-of-sale system to handle cash, check, and charge card
> transactions; need to track at least five hundred product codes,
> and be tied in to an inventory database so we'll know when we need to
> reorder. We will also need a computer, a modem, and a printer for or-
> dering new inventory and for processing online orders.

4. Production Processes: What types of production processes or activities will be needed to create products and prepare them for sale in a way that satisfies the success factors?

> Primary ongoing process is selecting and purchasing inventory,
> and creating attractive displays to present the merchandise.

5. Supply Chain: What relationships with suppliers and other providers will be required to run the venture and satisfy the success factors?

> Primary supply relationship would be with companies selling products
> to the store. A freelance designer will be needed to assist in design
> of displays for items such as commemorative T-shirts, buttons, post-
> ers, and cards.

6. Staffing: What type and level of staffing will be needed to operate this venture in a manner that meets the success factors?

> Gift shop will be open an average of 45 hours per week. Actual hours
> will be longer during our busiest seasons, and shorter when things are
> quieter. Will need a trained, skilled salesperson in the shop whenever
> it is open.

7. Key Ratios: What are the key operational and financial ratios that experienced managers in this industry track and manage to ensure success? What kinds of results does your research indicate you need to achieve with this venture?

> | | |
> |---|---|
> | Sales per visitor | $1.25–$1.75 |
> | Sales per square foot | $225–$275 |
> | Gross margin | 42%–47% |
> | Expenses (as % of net sales) | 35%–38% |
> | Inventory turnover | 2.5 times |

C. Pricing requirements

Your first look at pricing should consider three factors: customers, competition, and costs. For customers and competition, you will be able to draw on the information you've already gathered on those two topics earlier in this step. Costs will be covered in more detail in the financial analysis section of the feasibility study (Step 6). However, if you already know what your likely costs per unit will be, there is a place for that on Worksheet 5I.

Your conversations with target customers and those who are familiar with them probably suggested what these customers would be willing to pay for the product or service you are proposing to offer. This information should not be considered the last word, as most people are willing to pay more than what they say, but it's still useful to know.

Target customers may also have told you what similar products they currently purchase, which leads to looking at competitors' pricing. Often the most helpful data for identifying pricing requirements are the prices your primary competitors are charging.

By comparing what your target customers have said and what competitors are charging, you can usually come up with a reasonable set of pricing requirements. Note that these are not pricing decisions. You'll make some initial pricing assumptions to prepare the financial section of the feasibility study, and then make final pricing decisions as part of the business planning process in Step 7.

It's worth noting that nonprofits often strive to keep their prices low if not free, with the goal of making sure no one is denied access to their products or services. Ventures, on the other hand, require a different perspective. With a goal of earning income to cover costs or generate a profit, nonprofits recognize the need to set prices at a point that most, but not necessarily all, target customers will be willing to pay. The right price *should* lead to some complaints. No complaints probably means your prices are too low. So don't be concerned if as many as 10 percent of your prospective customers complain about your prices.[23] Take it as a compliment if people say your prices are high, but they go ahead and buy anyway.

Another useful perspective is to focus on value rather than price. Don't try to be the lowest-priced competitor but rather the one that delivers the greatest value in all the ways that matter to customers.

Finally, at this point, some organizations have already identified sales and profit goals for the proposed venture, and they wish to use those goals to inform the pricing analysis. Resist that urge, for now. You'll have the chance to state goals in the next step when you develop your feasibility financial analysis. Worksheet 5I: Pricing on page 223 helps you explore pricing issues. For this worksheet, focus on what customers, competition, and costs tell you about price. A sample is on page 98.

Identify the pricing requirements for this venture.

> Many nonprofits have a tendency to underprice their products and services, with the goal of making sure no one is denied access to them. Focus on value rather than price. Don't try to be the lowest-priced competitor but rather the one that delivers the greatest value.

WORKSHEET 5I   Pricing

Instructions

❑ With help from other members of your venture team, answer the following questions. Use Worksheet 5C: Customer Interest and Worksheet 5E: Competitor Profiles for necessary details.

❑ If you have difficulty answering the questions, you may need to do more market research.

Example: **Nature center gift shop**

1. Are there industry standards or practices that firms in this business tend to follow?

   ```
   The typical retail pricing strategy, known as keystoning,
   is to set prices equal to twice the wholesale cost. Thus, the cost
   for an item selling for $10 would be $5, which equals a 50% gross
   margin. Items such as t-shirts, jewelry, and a few gift categories
   generally allow for higher markups, while books, special sales and
   discounts (e.g., for members) generate smaller margins. Companies
   that order larger quantities can obtain lower wholesale costs.

   Other common pricing strategies include skimming (start high,
   reduce over time), penetration (start low, increase as demand
   builds), loss leaders (super low price to bring customers in), com-
   petitive (match others' prices), and bundling (sell multiple prod-
   ucts as a package). Most retailers utilize a combination of pricing
   strategies.
   ```

2. How do your primary competitors price their products? What can you ascertain about their pricing strategies?

   ```
   The Riverview Nature Center appears to use a formula for pricing
   their products. From what we've heard informally, they set most of
   their prices following the keystone (100% markup) strategy. Their
   average price is around $15. RNC does offer an assortment of propri-
   etary products (such as handcrafted items), which presumably allows
   for higher margins.

   The Discovery Channel stores appear to have an average price point
   in the $10-$15 range. By comparing several of their products with
   wholesale catalogs, we estimate that their gross margins vary from
   45% to 70%, depending on the item. They have several major sales
   each year, when their margins probably drop five to ten percentage
   points.
   ```

(continued)

> Birds of a Feather offers an eclectic mix of products that was hard to evaluate as a secret shopper. It seems that most items sell for $10 to $20. We also came across an article that indicated they have entered into an agreement with several other small shops to buy commodity items like birdseed together in order to take advantage of volume discounts.

3. What do your target customers appear willing to pay for your proposed products? You should be able to obtain this information from your answers to Worksheet 5C.

> Best evidence we have on this is the fact that visitors to other nature centers, whose profiles are similar to our own, tend to be willing to pay for gift shop items. Pricing, as noted elsewhere, needs to be moderate (average $10) with some higher end items.

4. What will it cost your organization to produce a product or service unit? (If this information is not readily available or requires some calculations, skip this question for now; details on how to calculate this can be found in the financials section of Step 6.)

> Based on discussions with nature center gift shop managers in other cities, we expect the product will cost, on average after discounts and sales, between 50% and 55% of what we sell it for.

5. Based on all of the above information, what would you state as the key pricing requirements for this venture idea?

> - Need to maintain an average item price of $10, with some unique, more expensive (and typically higher margin) products as well. Presentation of less expensive item bins near the entrance and near the cash register will support the perception that there is an even higher percentage of low-cost items.

> - Because a major portion of sales will come from children and families, we will make sure that there is an abundance of low-priced children's items.

D. Other requirements and approvals

Finally, your market research will usually uncover other operational requirements, such as legal or regulatory approvals. A thrift shop may need a building permit to build out its space; a refrigerator and air conditioner repair service might need an environmental permit to assure safe handling and disposal of toxic substances. All nonprofits need to confer with legal counsel to be sure ventures (and the proposed venture in particular) fit with the organization's legal structure, and to see if they will need to meet special legal requirements to protect the nonprofit's tax status. Worksheet 5J: Other Requirements and Approvals on page 225 helps you identify other operational approvals. A sample follows.

Identify any other requirements for this venture.

WORKSHEET 5J   Other Requirements and Approvals

Instructions

❑ Review the earlier worksheets in this step to see if any requirements have been missed.

❑ Using this information, and with help from other members of your venture team, answer the following questions.

❑ If you have difficulty answering the questions, you may need to do more market research.

Example: **Nature center gift shop**

1. What other requirements are needed to operate this venture?

   Building permit from the city will need to be pulled. Set up a system to receive and pay state and city sales taxes. Update the center's insurance plan to protect the shop against pilferage, product liability, and so on.

2. Has legal counsel informed you about any legal requirements that you need to be mindful of?

   Need to make sure that our products and marketing support the notion that this activity is related to our mission. All products need to have a nature or science theme that connects them with our displays and the natural environment. We will have to pay income taxes on any products that are not related to our mission.

Circulate the completed Step 5 worksheets to your venture team. With the team's help, decide whether the level of detail is sufficient, and whether the requirements you have identified offer a good match with your organization's core competencies. Present your findings to the entrepreneurial committee.

Circulate and discuss the completed Step 5 worksheets.

Step 5 summary

Step 5 is completed when you have solid information on the requirements to succeed with this venture, based on the market research you did for Worksheets 5A through 5F. As these requirements will play an essential role in preparing financial analysis, carefully check them over to verify you've answered all of the questions in sufficient detail. A good test is to see if your answers are presented with a level of detail similar to those in the examples.

The final question in this step is, Do these requirements fit well with your organization's core competencies and customers? Remember, this venture was selected, in part, because such a fit did seem to exist. So pull out your core competencies and customer worksheets, and decide whether the fit is still there. If it is, onward to Step 6!

From the research you've done, you now know much more about what it will take to make this venture successful. You have a good handle on who your target customers will be and what they want, what competition is to be expected, and how you will compare with those competitors. You have assessed what will be necessary for operating, pricing, and marketing the business. Next, in Step 6, you will use this information to create financial projections that predict the likely financial results from operating this venture.

Step 6: Prepare Feasibility Financial Analysis
How to use financial analysis to predict profitability

Time estimate:

Three to six weeks, 20 to 40 hours of work

Activity summary:

- Create an expense budget and calculate breakeven
- Prepare financial projections and evaluate risks
- Prepare feasibility recommendations

This is the point in the feasibility process where you translate your research into a budget and financial projections, and identify the uncertainties facing your venture. When you've completed this, you should have all the information needed to decide whether to commence this venture.

Financial projections are important for several reasons. First and foremost, they form the quantitative basis for evaluating the financial feasibility of your venture idea. Second, credible and conservative financial projections enable you to demonstrate the viability of the venture to the nonprofit's leadership, board, and funders. And, finally, if a decision is made to start the venture, these numbers form the basis for the business plan, which provides a tool for measuring, controlling, and evaluating how the venture is doing as time goes by.

Many project leaders bring in someone with financial skills when they reach Step 6. Some organizations have financial staff who can help with the financial projections. But you don't need to have an MBA or an accounting degree to work on this step. The first two parts, budgeting and breakeven analysis, do not require prior financial training, although some experience with budgeting would help. The third part, financial projections, does presume familiarity with standard financial reporting. This is where a project leader without financial training or experience might seek additional assistance. It's often a good idea to ask a finance person to look over the statements prepared for this step before you present them to the entrepreneurial committee. Many entrepreneurial committees include someone with financial expertise who might be willing to help out.

 Read Step 6, including all the worksheets and instructions. If needed, obtain additional expertise to complete this step.

There are four parts to feasibility financial analysis:

- Budgets
- Breakeven
- Projections
- Risks

Create an expense budget

Budgeting is where you determine what it will cost to start up and operate this venture. Remember, a key point of the requirements section in Step 5 was to identify the marketing and operational needs of the venture. In Step 6, you translate those requirements into budgets and financial projections.

First, calculate the costs associated with each of the identified requirements, as well as other costs that you know will exist even if they don't appear as a requirement. If current staff will operate the venture, be sure to include those costs in the budget also, in proportion to the time they will spend working on this venture. So far, this is basic budgeting, presumably similar to the process your nonprofit goes through to prepare its annual budget.

Second—and this is where the work goes beyond normal nonprofit budgeting—separate fixed costs from variable costs, as explained below:

- *Fixed costs.* These are direct costs that are incurred even if there are no sales. Examples include the cost to rent new space for the venture and the cost of new computer equipment, staff, and phone service. Some fixed costs are incurred on an annual basis (such as salaries). Other start-up expenses are not repeated for a number of years, such as computer equipment. For the latter, it's useful to know how long it will be before the cost will be incurred again. Many service businesses deliver services via permanent staff, which are fixed costs.

The question often comes up at this point as to whether indirect or overhead expenses should be included in the venture's budget. These costs typically include general operating expenses that the nonprofit incurs on an annual basis—such as rent or mortgage payments, administrative and accounting salaries, web site fees, and so forth—which support the whole organization. Many nonprofits allocate such expenses on a proportional basis; a typical approach is to assign overhead to each project or department as a percentage of direct expenses. For example, if Project X incurs $100,000 in direct expenses (such as staff salaries) and the percent needed to assign all indirect expenses is 20 percent (often called the overhead allocation formula), then Project X would have an annual expense budget equal to $120,000.

Now back to the question: should the budget for the proposed venture reflect a similar allocation? Many organizations say "yes, let's be consistent," and consider the matter closed. A more reasoned approach is to evaluate whether the allocation formula should be adjusted to fit the unique circumstances of the venture. Ventures are often evaluated on their financial performance in a way that an organization's other activities are not. At the same time, there is a tendency to foist so much overhead expense onto a newly proposed activity that it has no chance to get off the ground. In such an environment, good venture ideas can get smothered from allocated costs that a stand-alone business (such as one operated by a competitor) would not incur.

Some organizations get around this dilemma by adjusting the allocation percentage for the venture, while others agree to waive overhead for two or three years until the venture can get on its feet.

Fixed costs are new, direct costs that are incurred even if there are no sales. *Variable costs* are the costs that vary directly with how much the venture produces or sells.

Project Leader Tasks

❑ Read Step 6, including all worksheets and instructions.

❑ If needed, obtain additional expertise to complete this step.

❑ Prepare a budget (Worksheet 6A).

❑ Calculate breakeven (Worksheet 6B).

❑ Prepare financial projections (Worksheet 6C), risks (Worksheet 6D), and financial conclusions (Worksheet 6E).

❑ Present the results from Step 6 to the entrepreneurial committee.

❑ If the entrepreneurial committee recommends moving forward, request board approval to prepare a business plan to launch the venture.

A third approach is to assign full overhead for budgetary purposes, but then remove some or all of that allocation when evaluating the business. This "net internal value" calculation can also include other benefits that the venture provides to the nonprofit, such as covering expenses or providing services that the nonprofit would need to pay for if the venture did not exist. Whatever approach gets used, be sure to consider the unique characteristics of the venture before making your decision.

- *Variable costs.* These are the costs that vary directly with how much the venture produces or sells. It's a variable cost if, when you make or deliver more units, your total costs increase more or less in proportion to the number of units you make or sell. Examples include the costs of raw materials used to create products (or in retail, wholesale inventory costs) or the costs of contract labor for a service business. Variable costs are usually expressed in costs per unit produced or sold. Generally that's easier to calculate for a product than it is for a service, but it's important for both. The variable cost for a temporary employee service might include hourly wages for the temporary workers. Some costs include both fixed and variable elements, such as phone service that includes long distance calls. When this is the case, do your best to split the costs into their fixed (monthly phone service) and variable (long distance calls) categories.

Worksheet 6A: Budget on page 226 describes how to identify both kinds of costs for your venture idea. A sample follows.

Prepare a budget for this venture.

WORKSHEET 6A   Budget

Instructions

❏ Based on your research and the requirements worksheets in Step 5, create a one-year budget to start up and operate this venture.

❏ Next, separate out variable costs from fixed costs. For fixed costs, identify how long it will be before the cost will be incurred again.

Example: **Nonprofit exploring running focus groups as a venture**

1. What are the annual fixed costs to start up and operate this venture for one year?

   To make this calculation, first list each fixed cost along with its "useful life." For those costs that cover more than one year, enter only the first year's costs. To compute the first year's costs, divide the total cost by the number of years (its useful life). For example, if you pay $1,500 for a copy machine with a three-year life, you would assign $500 as the annual fixed cost. Expenses of this sort are often referred to as capital expenses.

   (Note: This is a simplified example to illustrate the concepts; your budget will probably contain more items.)

Fixed costs	Annual amount	Useful life in years
Salary of part-time coordinator	$20,000	annual
Technology purchases (computer, printer, phone, etc.)	$2,500	3 years
Marketing costs (brochures, mailings, conferences, etc.)	$4,000	annual
Space for coordinator and administrative suport	$6,000	annual
Total annual fixed costs	$32,500	

(continued)

2. What will the variable costs be for the products this venture will sell? You may need to make an assumption about average price per unit.

> Our research suggests an average price of $10,000 per customer, which will cover the whole focus group project including design, recruiting participants, facilitating three focus groups, and presenting a report to the client of the findings. Estimated variable costs for each unit (i.e., for a $10,000 project) would be:

Estimated variable cost	Cost
Facilitator fee	$1,500
Rent focus-group space (one-way mirrors, etc.)	$1,000
Commission paid to coordinator for the sale	$500
Food, parking, etc. for participants	$500
Total variable costs per unit	$3,500

3. Optional: Summarize fixed and variable costs graphically. Dollars form the vertical axis and sales units form the horizontal axis. Graph the fixed costs first; they will form a horizontal line. Graph the total costs next; they will form an ascending line rising above the fixed costs. The space between the fixed costs and the total costs is a graphic representation of variable costs.

Fixed and Variable Costs

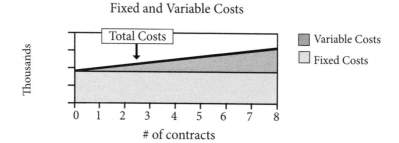

> Explanation of Graph: From question #1 above, fixed costs were calculated to be $32,500 and, per question #2, each contract adds $3,500 in variable costs to the budget. The point of distinguishing between fixed and variable costs, presented here both numerically and graphically, will become clear in the section on breakeven analysis.

Calculate breakeven

Breakeven, the quantity of annual sales needed to cover all costs, is a key benchmark that defines when the venture begins making money. Put simply, it says that you'll be losing money as long as sales are lower than breakeven, and you'll make a profit once sales exceed that level. It's worth noting that most new businesses do not break even until at least their second or third year of operation, and some require more years than that. The amount of money you expect to lose (including initial capital costs and cash flow requirements) before reaching breakeven represents the cost to start this venture. So you can see how important this calculation is.

Breakeven can be calculated using the following formula and data from Worksheet 6A: Budget.

> Breakeven = total annualized fixed costs / gross margin per unit

In this formula, gross margin per unit is simply the difference between what you charge for a product and what it costs you in variable costs to produce the unit.

Worksheet 6B: Breakeven Analysis on page 228, along with the sample on page 109, describes how to use this formula to calculate breakeven. Additional information on breakeven analysis, including what to do if your situation does not match the types of assumptions presented in the example, appears in Appendix F: Calculating Breakeven Using Percentage of Sales. Worksheet 6B uses what is known as the cost-per-average-unit method of calculating breakeven. For some venture ideas, the percentage-of-sales method described in the appendix works better.

Calculate breakeven for this venture.

Prepare financial projections

Financial projections build on the information you have collected, converting it into a format that will help you evaluate—and then implement—this venture idea. Ideally, preparing financial projections should be only slightly more difficult than doing a budget for a new program at your organization. The biggest difference for many nonprofits is calculating sales revenues. Your worksheets on customer interest, competitors, and requirements for operations, marketing, and pricing should help you with this task.

Financial projections can take many forms. Two pages of financial estimates work nicely for a simple venture idea, while more complicated ventures may require fifty pages. Your projections need to follow conventional accounting practices, and they should provide the level of detail required for your audience to review and evaluate them. Specifically, notes to the financial statements should be included. Notes enable the reader to determine how your figures were calculated. If you're working with a finance person from your organization, or with a financial consultant, her or she may have a preferred way to prepare these numbers that best suits your organization.

There is one thing to keep in mind as you prepare financial projections: Regardless of the audience for this report, you may feel pressure to come up with positive projections—to show that the venture will be profitable or at least break even. Nobody likes to see negative numbers in feasibility studies and business plans. Entrepreneurs tend to be optimists—at least when it comes to financial predictions—and you may feel you are expected to be one too. However, let the numbers speak for themselves. Resist the urge to *push* the data to get results that folks will feel good about.

> Regardless of the audience for this report, you may feel pressure to come up with positive projections—to show that the venture will be profitable or at least break even. Let the numbers speak for themselves. Resist the urge to *push* the data to get results that folks will feel good about.

If the evidence indicates start-up costs will be high and profits unlikely for a long time, report that. If you're not sure, be honest about that too. This is what it means to present *conservative* financial projections. It's not only honest to report the truth, but also it's best for the organization. Feasibility analysis should show how practical this venture idea is so that the organization can make the best decision. There's no point in taking on the risks of starting a venture if an objective review of the evidence suggests you shouldn't. When there is considerable uncertainty in the projections, especially on the sales side, many nonprofits will make two lists, one of optimistic assumptions and another of realistic assumptions, and then prepare separate financial projections for each list.

This is also the time to compare initial drafts of your financial projections with the sales and profit goals that your organization may have discussed earlier. Again, avoid "cooking" the numbers to create projections that people want to see. Instead, take a good second look at your assumptions, making adjustments as appropriate. Then, if the projections do not match expectations, clarify what can reasonably be expected (as opposed to wishful thinking) from this venture.

In most cases, financial projections include annual income and summary cash flow statements for the first three years, and a monthly detailed cash flow statement for the first year. Worksheet 6C: Financial Projections and Summary on page 231 presents a structure for gathering and utilizing your assumptions, and then shows how to prepare a summary based on the projections. A sample is on page 112.

Prepare financial projections for this venture.

WORKSHEET 6B   Breakeven Analysis

Instructions

❑ Pull out Worksheet 6A: Budget.

❑ Answer the questions to come up with an estimated breakeven for this venture idea.

❑ Do a "reality check" on the result (i.e., does this seem possible?) and on the supporting data (i.e., have you been realistic about costs?).

Example: **Focus groups**

1. What is the average unit price for your product? (From Worksheet 6A, question 2.)

   $10,000

2. What is the variable cost per unit? (From Worksheet 6A, question 2.)

   $3,500

3. What is the gross margin per unit?
   Gross margin per unit = average unit price - variable cost per unit

   $6,500 = $10,000 - $3,500

4. What are the estimated annual fixed costs for this product? (Worksheet 6A, question 1.)

   $32,500

5. Using the formula indicated below, when do you achieve breakeven? What does this tell you?
   Breakeven = total fixed costs / gross margin per unit

   5 units = $32,500 / $6,500

   Breakeven is 5 units or $50,000 (5 units x $10,000 average unit price) of sales.

   This shows that we need to sell five contracts per year at an average of $10,000 each, or $50,000 in total sales, in order to break even. We begin to make a profit starting with the sixth contract, or for sales beyond $50,000.

(continued)

6. Check your results by calculating profit if sales equal breakeven. If sales equal the breakeven quantity, profits should be zero (or close to zero depending on rounding errors).

	Units	Cost
Total sales	**5 units x $10,000**	$50,000
Less total variable costs	**5 units x $3,500**	$17,500
Gross margin		$32,500
Less total fixed costs		$32,500
Profit (loss)		$0

7. Estimate profit and loss if you sell quantities greater or less than breakeven. What does this tell you?

	Units If we sell 3	Cost	Units If we sell 8	Cost
Total sales at $ **10,000** per unit	3 x $10,000	$30,000	8 x $10,000	$80,000
Less total variable costs at $ **3,500** per unit	3 x $3,500	$10,500	8 x $3,500	$28,000
Gross margin		$19,500		$52,000
Less total fixed costs		$32,500		$32,500
Profit (loss)		($13,000)		$19,500

If we sell eight units or $80,000 worth of focus groups, our profit is $19,500. On the other hand if we sell only three units or $30,000, we lose $13,000. This tells us we should be confident we can sell at least five focus groups per year—probably six or seven to be on the safe side—before deciding to start this venture. It also suggests that, if possible, our fixed cost should be lower - perhaps we'll hold off on some of the expenses until we get enough customers lined up to justify them.

(continued)

8. Optional: Present profits and losses graphically. Dollars form the vertical axis and units sold form the horizontal axis. Graph the fixed costs, the total costs, and the sales. (Use the graphic created in Worksheet 6A as a starting point.) The point at which the sales line crosses over the variable costs line represents the beginning of profitability.

Breakeven Point

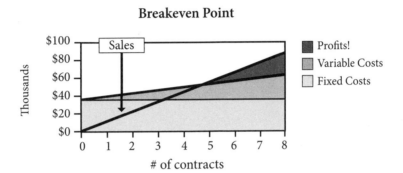

Explanation of graph: This graph shows fixed costs as a horizontal line—a constant $32,500 per year regardless of the number of contracts sold. The variable costs start at zero in relation to the fixed costs and increase at the rate of $3,500 per contract. Sales are shown as a third line, increasing in $10,000 increments for each contract sold. The graph shows that breakeven occurs at 5 contracts, or $50,000 of sales. Profits occur when more than five contracts are sold.

9. Reality check: Do these results seem plausible? It's all right if you don't know, but if the numbers seem outside the range of possibility, now is the time to evaluate whether to proceed to the next worksheet. Similarly, are you confident that you have been realistic about costs? One way to measure this: Do you have about as much confidence in this budget as you have in your nonprofit's annual budget (or your department, if that's a better comparison)?

   Since we've already run a number of focus groups, we are pretty confident about the costs. And while we're less certain on the sales side—can we sell them for an average of $10,000 each—our market research showed this is a competitive price for companies that do this kind of work.

WORKSHEET 6C   Financial Projections and Summary

Instructions

❑ **Revenues:** Based on your previous research, what's a conservative estimate of sales for each of the first three years of operations?

❑ **Costs:** Taking the costs you identified in Worksheets 6A and 6B, what do you estimate those costs will be for each of the first three years?

❑ **Projections:** With help from a finance person (if needed), prepare an initial draft of your financial projections using a computer spreadsheet program. Be sure to prepare a cash flow statement as well as an income statement. Discuss them with your venture team, and then make adjustments as appropriate.

❑ **Financing:** Based on your projections, how much financing will be required to launch and operate this venture for its first three years?

❑ **Notes:** Prepare notes to your financial statements, listing your assumptions and how you calculated your projections.

Examples of these statements and a summary appear below, and notes to these statements appear in Appendix D: Sample Financial Plan for Nature Center Gift Shop.

Example: **Nature center gift shop**

Financial Summary

Income Statement	2002-03	% of sales	2003-04	% of sales	2004-05	% of sales
Sales	$85,000*	100%	$140,000	100%	$160,000	100%
Cost of goods sold (COGS)						
• Merchandise	$45,050	53%	$74,200	53%	$84,800	53%
• Freight	$1,700	2%	$2,800	2%	$3,200	2%
Total COGS	$46,750	55%	$77,000	55%	$88,000	55%
Gross margin (sales – COGS)	$38,250	45%	$63,000	45%	$72,000	45%
Other income (such as grants)	$0		$0		$0	

*Partial year (9 months). Store opens October 1, 2002.

(continued)

Worksheet 6C—Financial Projections and Summary

Income Statement (continued)	2002-03	% of sales	2003-04	% of sales	2004-05	% of sales
Expenses						
• Operating expenses	$3,000	4%	$4,000	3%	$4,500	3%
• Salaries & fringe	$43,920	52%	$47,504	34%	$50,560	32%
• Interest expense	$3,600	4%	$2,880	2%	$2,160	1%
• Depreciation	$2,200	3%	$2,200	2%	$2,200	1%
Total expenses	$52,720	62%	$56,584	40%	$59,420	37%
Profit (gross margin - total expenses)	($14,470)	-17%	$6,416	5%	$12,580	8%

Sales and profit projections

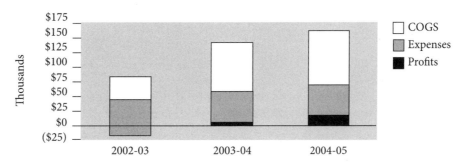

(continued)

Worksheet 6C—Financial Projections and Summary

Summary Cash Flow Analysis	2002–03	2003–04	2004–05
Beginning cash balance	$0	$3,137	$503
+ Add loan proceeds	$45,000		
− Deduct captial expense (build-out)	($11,000)		
+ Add sales revenue	$85,000	$140,000	$160,000
− Deduct inventory purchases and freight	($65,343)**	($77,000)	($88,000)
− Deduct expenses	($52,720)	($56,584)	($59,420)
+ Add depreciation	$2,200	$2,200	$2,200
− Deduct principal payments	$0	($11,250)	($11,250)
Ending cash balance	$3,137	$503	$4,033

**Includes approximately $19,000 for purchase of initial inventory

Financial Summary

The gift shop is projected to generate sales of $85,000 during its first year, 2002-03 (partial year), increasing to $160,000 by year three. The gift shop is expected to lose $14,470 in the first year, and recover $6,416 of that in year two. In the third year it is projected to earn a profit of $12,580.

A bank loan of $45,000 will be needed in July 2002 to build out the space ($11,000), purchase initial inventory ($19,000), and for working capital ($15,000). The loan will be repaid over a five-year period.

It is projected that during year one the gift shop will need additional working capital to cover monthly cash flow requirements. See detailed monthly cash flow statement [Appendix D]. For that reason, the gift shop is expected to draw upon a no-interest, internal working capital line of credit of $7,000.

Evaluate risks

At this point it is important to step back and consider the uncertainties you face by starting this venture. Certainly the most obvious one for most start-ups is the risk that sales will not achieve estimated levels or that costs turn out higher than anticipated. At its extreme, this concern includes the risk that you've read the market wrong or that you won't be able to adequately market the service, and sales will never reach breakeven.

Here are other risks to consider:

- IRS scrutiny may increase (more likely for nonprofits with ventures)
- Management attention and time may be distracted by the venture
- Some current funders may not share your enthusiasm for ventures
- Negative publicity may be generated by private businesses complaining of unfair competition

Worksheet 6D: Risks on page 233 guides you and the venture team as you identify uncertainties. A sample is on page 117.

Identify risks with this venture.

Prepare findings and recommendations

The final task in the feasibility process is to decide whether the evidence supports developing this idea into a venture.

There are essentially two questions at this point in the process, each of which is addressed using the work you've done on the previous worksheets:

1. Can we make money from this?
2. Are we comfortable with the risks and uncertainties?

A yes for these two questions typically leads to the decision to proceed to Step 7—writing a business plan to launch this venture.

Don't be surprised if you find some problems with your venture idea. A thorough feasibility study always comes up with problems—and no business operates without them. Be careful not to ignore problems; paying attention to them now will be far more beneficial to your organization than ignoring them. And indeed, since this is a feasibility study, keep yourself open to the possibility that this is not such a great venture idea after all.

Don't be surprised if you find some problems with your venture idea. A thorough feasibility study always comes up with problems—and no business operates without them.

The feasibility study is not a grant proposal. Remember that rejecting impractical ideas is as important and as valuable as finding good ones. Entrepreneurs say they learn as much from their mistakes as they do from their successes. A carefully executed feasibility study should help you learn some of those lessons, and you'll do so at a fraction of the cost of making them in the marketplace! Moreover, the time you spend on a poor idea will not be wasted. You will have learned much about researching feasibility. As the approach can be used for the next venture idea to be considered, it will take less time to evaluate the next venture.

Worksheet 6E: Financial Conclusions on page 236 describes how to address the two questions listed above. A sample is on page 121.

Prepare financial conclusions. After completing Worksheet 6E, write up your conclusions and recommendations, and discuss them with your venture team. Present your completed feasibility study (Steps 5 and 6) to your entrepreneurial committee. If the committee decides to recommend a decision to launch this venture idea, present this recommendation to your board and request approval.

Step 6 summary

In Step 6, you translated the data from your research into financial projections. Based on those projections and your other findings, the entrepreneurial committee and the board weighed in on whether this venture has sufficient merit to write a business plan. If the answer was yes, then you're ready to move on to Step 7.

Chapter Three Summary

A positive outcome to Steps 5 and 6 provides you with the confidence that this venture idea represents a promising opportunity for your organization and helps you decide to start the venture. You now know much more about your customers, your competitors, and the industry than you did before you started the feasibility steps. That knowledge will be very important as you write the business plan and begin operating this venture.

WORKSHEET 6D   Risks

Instructions

❏ Meet with your venture team to discuss risks and uncertainties.

❏ List in this worksheet those that seem most significant.

Example: **Nature center gift shop**

1. What risk will you face if sales are lower than anticipated? What would happen if sales were down 10 percent or even 25 percent from your projections?

> As a start-up venture, the gift shop does not have a prior sales history to utilize for making projections. Instead, we're relying on circumstantial evidence (e.g., industry data) that sufficient numbers of our visitors will become gift shop customers. It's certainly possible that sales will not equal projections, or it will take longer than expected to reach these sales targets.

> Lower sales would of course adversely impact profits. Assuming 45% gross margins, every $1,000 decrease in sales will result in a $450 decline in profits. (This assumes constant operating costs.)

> The impact on profits of a 10%, 25% and 50% shortfall in sales in 2003-04 would be as follows:

Impact of a sales shortfall in 2003-04

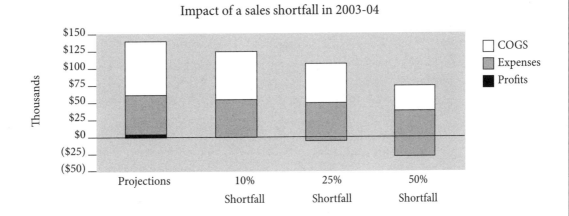

(continued)

	Projections	10% sales shortfall	25% sales shortfall	50% sales shortfall
Net sales	$140,000	$126,000	$105,000	$70,000
Cost of goods	$77,000	$69,300	$57,750	$38,500
Expenses	$56,584	$56,584	$56,584	$56,584
Profit (loss)	$6,416	$116	($9,334)	($25,084)

Thus, the impact of a 10% sales shortfall in 2003-04 would be to reduce a $6,000 profit nearly to zero. For the second year in business, that might be acceptable. However, a 25% shortfall would generate a $9,000 loss, which would be a problem, and a 50% shortfall, causing a $25,000 loss, would be a much bigger problem. We believe a 50% shortfall is unlikely, but cannot rule out the possibility of a 10%-25% shortfall. Of course, actual results could also exceed the projections.

2. What is the risk that costs will be higher than expected? Consider both variable and fixed costs.

We have a good handle on wholesale prices for the products that would be sold in the shop, based on supplier catalogs and discussions with managers of other gift shops. But there is a risk that our gross margins, projected at 45%, will in fact be lower as a result of more discounts and sales than projected. A 5% reduction in gross margins would turn the $6,000 projected profit in 2003-04 into a small loss.

On the fixed cost side, the largest expense would be for staff, with smaller expenses for marketing, interest, and depreciation. We're confident that these costs will not turn out to be higher than projected.

(continued)

3. What is the risk that prices you have assumed are too high, and that you'll need to reduce your prices to attract customers and remain competitive?

> We're generally comfortable about this risk also, again based on shopping a variety of gift shops and meeting with other gift shop managers. As long as we keep our average price low, and have plenty of low-priced (under $10) items in the shop, this risk should be minimal.

4. What are the risks if it proves difficult to attract suitable workers for this venture?

> Our mission and natural setting has helped us attract top-notch staff to work at the nature center despite salaries below prevailing levels. We're expecting this to work for the gift shop also, but there is some uncertainty on that point. Frequent turnover in staffing the gift shop would undermine success.

> The risk is that it will be difficult to attract and retain qualified gift shop staff, forcing us to reduce hours or utilize unqualified staff. Given our projections, increasing wages significantly to attract workers would likely make the business untenable.

5. What other important risks and uncertainties can you anticipate? How serious are these risks?

> Several come to mind. None represent major barriers but each will require attention: (1) While the advice we've gotten is that the best way to promote the gift shop is by integrating it into other nature center activities (e.g., mention it in all nature center publications, start and end naturalist tours at the gift shop), that will not come easy for some staff. The risk is that the gift shop will be seen as something different and apart from the nature center, and as a result will not receive the kind of internal support it needs to attract customers.

> (2) There is a risk that, as a nonprofit with a strong sense of mission, we will look for products that we think people should have rather than ones that they will want. (3) Lastly, the gift shop will rely almost exclusively on nature center visitors as its source for customers. If those numbers should decline, even temporarily, the financial impact on the gift shop would be significant.

(continued)

6. Among the risks indicated above, which are the most serious?

> ```
> First, that sales will not reach projected levels, and second,
> that gross margins will be lower than projected. We're fairly
> confident about the other risks indicated above.
> ```

7. If the venture's financial results were significantly worse than projected, what would be done? What steps would be taken to reduce costs? At what point would the venture be shut down? How difficult (financially and otherwise) would that be for the organization?

> ```
> We'd cut our expenses by reducing operating and staffing hours,
> and by carrying a smaller inventory. Our purpose with this ven-
> ture is both mission-related (additional mechanism to inform and
> support appreciation of the natural world) and financial (gener-
> ate funds to support the mission). So we would regularly evaluate
> the shop's impact in both areas; any decision on closing it would
> have to consider both impacts.
> ```

> ```
> Finally, we intend to take a long-term perspective on this. We
> would most likely continue operating the gift shop even if ini-
> tial financial results turned out to be worse than projected, if
> we had good reason to conclude that the financial targets were
> still achievable but would take longer to reach.
> ```

WORKSHEET 6E   Financial Conclusions

Instructions

❑ Pull out your Worksheet 6C: Financial Projections and Summary and Worksheet 6D: Risks.

❑ Prepare written summaries as requested in this worksheet.

Example: **Nature center gift shop**

1. What are your sales and profit projections for the first three years operating this venture idea? (Retrieve from Worksheet 6C.)

   The gift shop is projected to generate sales of $85,000 during its first year, 2002-03 (partial year), increasing to $160,000 by year three. The gift shop is expected to lose $14,470 in the first year, and recover $6,416 of that in year two. In the third year it is projected to earn a profit of $12,580.

   A bank loan of $45,000 will be needed in July 2002 to build out the space ($11,000), purchase initial inventory ($19,000), and for working capital ($15,000). The loan will be repaid over a five-year period.

2. What are the most important underlying factors driving these numbers?

   Growth will be driven primarily by increased visibility of the gift shop and by expected increases in attendance at the center.

3. How confident are you that these results can be achieved? What's the margin of uncertainty?

   Sales estimates were developed from reviewing actual results from gift shops in similar nature centers. While there is uncertainty, a review of our estimates by a consultant in the field and by a gift shop manager at another nature center in Ohio suggests our estimates are reasonable, if not conservative.

4. What are the most significant risks and uncertainties facing this venture idea? Why do you believe these uncertainties either will not occur or can be overcome?

   That sales will not reach projected levels. See answer to previous question.

5. Based on all of your feasibility analysis (Steps 5 and 6), does the evidence support a conclusion that this venture appears sufficiently feasible to justify a decision to write a business plan to commence operations?

   Yes.

Chapter Four

Business Planning

Business planning turns your business *idea* into a business *operation*. The business plan shows that you know what needs to be done to start and run a successful venture. You began work on it when you collected information for the feasibility study in Steps 5 and 6. Most of the analysis is over; now it's time to make decisions such as who will run the venture, where it will carry out operations, and how it will be operated and marketed.

Here's the good news. Your business plan does not have to be a huge treatise. It can take a variety of forms—a simple action plan, your completed worksheets, or a formal written document—depending on how your business plan will be used and the results of your feasibility study. If you did all the feasibility work in Chapter Three, then you have 75 percent of the information you will need for the business plan. Much of writing the business plan entails converting the marketing, operational, pricing, and other venture requirements you identified in Chapter Three into implementation plans. For example, the feasibility research for an elder personal care services venture revealed a marketing requirement to promote this service to key referral networks such as human resources (HR) directors at large employers. The business plan then described precisely what promotional activities would be done to meet this requirement: build a mailing list of HR directors and referral agencies, contact them to get on their preferred referral lists, create appealing brochures, and so on.

By the end of this chapter, you will transform your thorough research (done in Chapter Three) into a business plan that gives you and your organization the confidence to proceed with the venture. You will know that you have investigated all the relevant issues facing your new venture.

Step 7: Write a Business Plan
How to create a road map for business success

Time estimate:

Four to eight weeks, 30 to 60 hours of work

Activity summary:

- Identify the people who will be in charge and the audience for the plan
- Write the business plan; make final decisions on marketing, operations, and finance
- Get the plan approved

Does every business need a formal business plan? Many successful businesses start without one, and many nonprofit ventures don't need one either. Sometimes all you need is a simple action plan and a budget. If your feasibility study was unambiguously positive, and you can answer each of the following questions with an equally unambiguous yes, then you can get by with a simple action plan:

- Your nonprofit already has extensive experience with the target customers. That experience indicates that the marketing required to entice sufficient numbers will be fairly straightforward and inexpensive.

- Your nonprofit's experience demonstrates a solid ability to produce, distribute, and price your product in a manner that will attract these customers. Furthermore, your organization already makes the proposed product, or the product is not much different from what the nonprofit is already doing.

- The costs and risks of starting this activity are nominal, requiring minimal internal start-up investments and no external financing.

If your answers indicate that a simple action plan will suffice, prepare the following additions to your feasibility study, obtain the approvals you need, and get started. The feasibility study indicated most of what you need to know about the opportunity, and the rest you'll learn from experience. Many businesses start just this way, and there's nothing wrong with it. All you need to do is

- Identify responsibilities and authority
- Identify the action steps and timeline to launch and manage the business
- Prepare a simple budget

An example would be a nonprofit counseling service that decides to charge for a new service requested by many clients—couples counseling. This activity could be initiated using existing staff. Such a change might be straightforward enough to require only a quick market study and a simple action plan. The plan might include estimates of costs to print and mail new brochures, revisions to the web site, and a list of referral sources. Finally, it would project expected new business from this new service offering. Action steps would include deciding on pricing (using the market and competitor analysis from the feasibility step), identifying the employees who will carry out these steps, and establishing a timeline. Preparation of a full business plan for this activity would not be worth the investment in staff time.

But in most other situations, a business plan will be necessary. You will need one when the feasibility study indicates that *any* of the following conditions exist:

- Outside financing or significant internal resources will be required.

- Marketing to the target market will be a stretch, either because your nonprofit has not done a venture in this market before or because your nonprofit will need to use unfamiliar strategies and techniques.

- The venture carries risks that could threaten the nonprofit's other programs—valuable programs might have to be shut down if the venture failed.

- Management, marketing, operations, or financial projections for this venture are sufficiently complex that planning is required beyond the feasibility study.

- The board of directors insists that a business plan be written for any venture.

The tone of a business plan should be positive and confident, in contrast to the analytical skepticism of a feasibility study. Business plans typically make assertions with unambiguous certainty, such as "we will achieve sales of $100,000."

Project Leader Tasks

❑ Read Step 7, including all the worksheets and instructions.

❑ Identify the person who will be charged with starting and running this venture. Assign that person to writing the business plan. Begin by using the feasibility worksheets from Steps 5 and 6 and other information you have collected to fill in what is already known for each worksheet in this step.

❑ Prepare Worksheets 7A: Business Plan Audience, 7B: Business Summary, 7C: The Opportunity, and 7D: The People.

❑ Prepare implementation plans using Worksheets 7E: Operational Plan, 7F: Marketing Plan, 7G: Start-up Plan, 7H: Financial Plan, and 7I: Contingencies.

❑ Circulate the completed Step 7 worksheets to your venture team.

❑ Finish the business plan. If necessary for the audience, convert completed worksheets into a formal written document.

❑ Secure approvals (including financing if needed).

❑ Start the venture!

Identify the person who will be in charge of the venture

A business plan is an action plan that clearly states who will take responsibility for implementing it—who will convert it from paper into action. *It is not a business plan until it indicates who will be in charge of the venture.*

Consequently, the first task in Step 7 is to decide who will be in charge of this venture and to get that person to decide who will be on the team working on this venture. These are probably the most important decisions to make while preparing the business plan. Select or hire someone who has the time, the inclination, and the expertise to run this venture. In most cases, volunteers do not represent a good choice for overseeing the venture.

Once you've decided who will be in charge of this venture, have him or her prepare the business plan. Business success depends heavily on developing mutually rewarding relationships with customers, suppliers, and staff, and on a solid understanding of the issues involved in this venture. Get the people who will develop that understanding and those relationships working on the business plan as soon as possible. A business opportunity is not a good one until you have the right people lined up to run it.

> The plan is not a business plan until it indicates who will be in charge of the venture.

If the venture manager is not on board yet, an alternative is the person who will hire and supervise the manager. This person needs to take on the writing task as if he or she will be responsible for implementing it. Sometimes a consultant can help organize and write the plan, as long as the staff person responsible for implementation is closely involved with the work and makes all the key business planning decisions.

Identify who will be in charge of this venture. Make that *person responsible for preparing the business plan.*

The next activity in writing a good business plan is identifying the audience for the plan. This issue is addressed in Worksheet 7A: Business Plan Audience on page 238. A sample is on page 128.

Identify the audience for the business plan.

The five essential sections of a business plan

The five essential business plan sections are

1. Business Summary
2. Market Opportunity
3. People
4. Implementation
5. Contingencies

Once you've completed the worksheets, you will have the information you need to complete your business plan. Indeed, for internal review of most venture ideas, presenting the worksheets themselves along with financial projections might be sufficient. But if you plan to seek financing, you'll want to convert the worksheets into a more formal written document.

- The **Business Summary** briefly describes your organization and the proposed venture. It summarizes in one or two pages the key information and conclusions that appear in the rest of the business plan, including who will be running it, how it will be operated, marketed, and financed, and how you are prepared for the unexpected.

- The **Market Opportunity** section concisely describes the venture, what it will sell to whom, how it will be profitable, what competition it will face, and how fast it will grow and why.

- The **People** section is arguably the most important part of the business plan. Who will be responsible for developing, marketing, and operating this venture? Why are they the right people to make sure this venture will be successful? What experience and expertise do they have that is directly related to this opportunity?

- **Implementation** is the "how-to" section of the business plan. This is where the action steps get clarified in four key areas—marketing, operations, start-up, and financials. Most nonprofits find that the biggest hole at this point in the process is developing their implementation plans, particularly in the marketing area.

- The **Contingencies** section identifies factors that could hinder venture success, such as ineffective marketing, unexpected costs, or difficulty attracting suitable staff. It also describes management's plans to address those factors.

Tips and worksheets for each of these sections follow. Be sure to first read through to the end of this chapter to get a feel for the questions you will be answering. As you fill out the remaining worksheets, keep in mind the audience you determined in Worksheet 7A.

Section I: Business summary

Tips for writing this section:

- Draft rough answers to Worksheet 7B prior to starting the remaining worksheets in this step. This will help reveal any gaps in your information.

- Once you've finished the other worksheets in this chapter, you can return and finish this one.

Write a summary of the business.

WORKSHEET 7A   Business Plan Audience

Instructions

❑ Identify the audience for the business plan. Whose approval will be needed before the venture can be launched?

❑ Write down what they will be looking for in the plan; if you're uncertain, ask them.

Example: **Nature center gift shop**

1. Who is the audience for this business plan?

   Executive director, controller, board of directors, and local bank managers (for the loan).

2. What will they be looking for in the plan?

   Executive director said he will be looking for evidence that sales projections are reasonable and based on facts, not hope. Controller expects the business plan to be thorough in anticipating costs, so that there will be few surprises after we start the venture.

   Board perspective varies by individual, but our overall sense is that they want to make sure we won't be putting the programs at risk, by diverting staff and resources away from the nature center.

   Banker wants to feel confident we know what we're doing; she is as interested in who we will be hiring to manage the gift shop as what is in the business plan.

3. How will they evaluate the plan?

   Mostly boils down to whether we've done all of our homework, and whether the benefits (dollars and mission-related) justify the costs including staff time.

4. Who will be responsible for preparing the business plan? What are his or her qualifications to do this work?

   Jackie Olson, who will be hired as the store manager once the business plan is approved and financing secured, will prepare the business plan. We've contracted with her to write the busi-ness plan on a consulting ba-sis. She has extensive experience in retailing, and is currently a vol-unteer naturalist at the nature center.

WORKSHEET 7B   Business Summary

Instructions

❑ Pull out your completed worksheets for Steps 5 and 6.

❑ Fill out what you can below; return to fill in the gaps once you've finished
the remaining worksheets in Step 7.

Example: **Nature center gift shop**

1. Summarize the nonprofit's mission, services, and role in the community.

> **The Prairie Flower Nature Center, founded in 1975, seeks to
> increase public awareness and understanding of the natural envi-
> ronment through educational and sensory experiences with nature.
> The nature center owns 250 acres of undeveloped land and wetlands
> adjacent to a major metropolitan area, with nature trails, natu-
> ralist tours, a model farm, and a wildflower demonstration gar-
> den. Its 5,000-square-foot visitor center contains classrooms, a
> nature lab with microscopes, animal touch boxes, and other hands-
> on exhibits of prairie and forest displays of interest to both
> children and adults. It is recognized as the premier facility of
> its kind in the region.**

> **Its programs attract approximately 120,000 visitors each year,
> including 60,000+ K-12 school children, who participate in edu-
> cational programs that meet state educational standards and are
> taught by qualified naturalists. Because of the center's national
> reputation for songbirds and prairie flowers, and creative pro-
> grams and exhibits, it attracts out-of-town tourists as well as
> local visitors.**

> **The Prairie Flower Nature Center is funded from entrance fees
> and contributions from governmental, corporate, and individual
> sources.**

2. What prior experience and expertise does the nonprofit have—in terms of core competencies,
resources, and management and marketing capabilities—to operate a successful venture? To help
with this question, refer to the information gathered for Step 2, Conduct a Venture Audit.

> **The natural beauty of the parklands, the attractive yet earthy design
> of the visitor center, and, most important, its exhibits and knowl-
> edgeable staff and naturalists enable it to attract large numbers of
> visitors. They will provide a key source of customers for the proposed
> gift shop.**

(continued)

The center's expertise and reputation in nature-based programs, work-shops, and educational curriculum will assure customers of the authenticity and quality of merchandise available for purchase in the gift shop.

3. In a nutshell, what is this business all about? Who will the customers be, and what evidence is there that they will be willing to pay for something like this? Most of this information can be found in your feasibility research. (Summarize from Worksheets 5B and 5C.)

The shop will offer retail items with a nature or science theme for adults and children in a number of categories, including books, clothing, posters, CDs and videos, gifts, equipment for outdoor pursuits such as hiking, birding, and gardening, and stuffed animals, toys, and educational material. The shop will also specialize in birding supplies and prairie/native plants gardening to complement the center's expertise. Near the shop will be an area with tables and chairs that offers light refreshments for sale such as soda, spring water, pastries, and ice cream.

Customers will be drawn primarily from those attending the center. Evidence of customer interest includes successful gift shops at other nature centers, industry data on average sales per visitor and sales per square foot for other gift shops, and the existence of a growing number of independently owned retail shops that carry nature-related merchandise.

This venture has both an educational and financial purpose. The educational purpose is to further our educational mission by developing an additional mechanism to inform and support appreciation of the natural world. The financial purpose is to generate funds to support that mission. Proceeds will be used to preserve and enhance the natural and educational resources of the nature center.

4. Who will manage, market, and operate this venture? Why will their backgrounds and experience ensure its success?

A person with more than ten years experience in gift shop retailing will manage this venture. In addition, an assistant manager will be hired.

(continued)

Worksheet 7B—Business Summary

5. What revenues do you expect from this venture? When do you expect to reach breakeven and at what sales volume level? What will it cost (start-up expenses plus initial losses) to get to that point? How profitable will it become? (Retrieve from Worksheet 6C.)

> The gift shop is projected to generate sales of $85,000 during its first and partial year, 2002-03, increasing to $160,000 by year three. The gift shop is expected to lose $14,470 in the first year, and recover $6,416 of that in year two. In the third year it is projected to earn a net profit of $12,580.
>
> A bank loan of $45,000 will be needed in July 2002 to build out the space ($11,000), purchase initial inventory ($19,000), and for working capital ($15,000). The loan will be repaid over a five-year period.

6. What are the most significant risks that could undermine success with this venture, and what will be done to overcome them?

> The major risk is that product selection and presentation will not match up with customer expectations, leading to lower than expected sales. To overcome that concern, we have developed a careful process for frequent product review and testing. Secondly, there could be fewer visitors than expected, which could translate into lower sales at the gift shop. If this occurred, the gift shop would take steps to increase average sales per customer.

Section II: Market opportunity

Tips for writing this section:

- Here's where you provide a detailed description of what you plan to provide (your products or services), to whom you will provide it (your target customers), and why they will purchase this from you (rather than your competitors).

- Most of these answers can be obtained from the worksheets you completed in Steps 5 and 6, although you will need to edit and adapt them.

Worksheet 7C: The Opportunity on page 242 will help you write this section of your business plan. A sample is on page 132.

Describe the opportunity presented by this venture.

WORKSHEET 7C   The Opportunity

Instructions

❑ Pull out your completed worksheets for Steps 5 and 6.

❑ Cut and paste, editing as needed, to complete this worksheet.

Example: **Nature center gift shop**

1. What products will be sold via this venture? (Retrieve from Worksheet 5B, question 2.)

> **The gift shop will offer retail items with a nature or science theme for adults and children in a number of categories, including gifts, jewelry, books, clothing, posters, CDs and videos, equipment for outdoor pursuits such as hiking, birding, and gardening, and stuffed animals, toys, and educational material. The shop will specialize in birding supplies and prairie/native plants gardening to complement the center's expertise. Near the shop will be an area with tables and chairs that offers light refreshments for sale such as soda, spring water, pastries, and ice cream.**

2. Who are the target customers for these products? Be specific. Compare and contrast the various customer groups that will be targeted. What benefits will these customers perceive from purchasing these products? (Retrieve from Worksheet 5B, question 1.)

Customer segment	Description	
Nature enthusiasts (includes our members)	Profile:	**Emotional tie to nature, enjoy native birds and wildflowers. Typically 40-65 in age, suburban, middle income. Often tend nature gardens and bird feeders at home. About 20% are families with children under 18. About 5% are tourists (live 100+ miles away).**
	Size:	**Of our 120,000 annual visitors, about 20,000 are in this segment. Center currently has 1,200 members ($25 individual, $38 family), who visit the center an average of three times per year.**
	Trend:	**Growing**
	Benefits:	**Information and items to enhance their experience with nature.**

(continued)

Customer segment		Description
Casual nature strollers	Profile:	**Enjoy nature (and nature centers) as just another outdoor activity. Typically somewhat younger (25-50) than nature enthusiasts, also middle income and suburban. About 50% are families with children under 18.**
	Size:	**Account for about 40,000 of our visitors.**
	Trend:	**Stable**
	Benefits:	**Impulsive gift buying if something catches their attention.**
School and scout groups	Profile:	**Outdoor, educational activity organized by teachers or scout leaders. Grades 4-9. 50% suburban, 40% urban, 10% rural.**
	Size:	**About 60,000 children visit the center each year as part of a school or scout group.**
	Trend:	**Fast growth**
	Benefits:	**Teachers/scout leaders: supports educational objectives. Children: enjoy being outdoors, collecting stuffed animals, toys, and plastic bugs.**

**Strategies for attracting each of these groups will be
described in the marketing section of this business plan.**

3. Detail the *evidence* demonstrating that the target customers will be interested in purchasing these products. (Summarize from Worksheet 5C, question 1.)

**Our successful sales of books, reproductions, and posters during
special events at the nature center. From our member survey and visitor interviews, 64% of members and 33% of visitors say they'd become
gift shop customers.**

(continued)

Name	Nature center visitors	Store size (sq. ft.)	Sales	Sales/ visitor	Sales/ square feet
Big Woods Conservation Park	90,000	700	$135,000	$1.50	$193
Douglas Science Museum	130,000	650	$205,000	$1.58	$315
Great Lakes Interpretive Center	80,000	750	$175,000	$2.19	$233
Mississippi Flyway Center	120,000	600	$160,000	$1.33	$267
Averages	–	–	–	$1.65	$252

4. Who else is successfully selling similar products to comparable target customers that suggests this could be successful? (Also from Worksheet 5C, question 1.)

   Data from four nature centers closest to ours in size and attendance are as follows:

   Three of these centers said their gift shops are profitable; the fourth just opened their gift shop a year ago. According to the Museum Store Association, the average gift shop for a nature center of our size generates gross margins equal to 45% of net sales.

5. What trends in the marketplace provide further evidence that you will be able to sell these products to these customers? (Summarize from Worksheet 5C, question 2.)

   An increasing number of nature centers have gift shops. Some nature-oriented nonprofits operate mail-order catalogs. A recent opening in our metropolitan area of a second Discovery Channel store, which sells science and nature items with an emphasis on children's products, also suggests this is a growing market. Press reports indicate this company is profitable and continues to grow.

(continued)

Plant nurseries specializing in nature plants and stores devoted to bird feeding and birding have opened in our area recently. Shelf space devoted to these topics at local bookstores increases each year. Local libraries have noted greater interest in these topics as well.

6. How many customers and how much in annual sales will you obtain from these customers? (Retrieve from Worksheet 5C, question 3.)

Given our 120,000 total annual visitors, and using industry data from similarly sized nature centers that suggest sales of $1.50 per visitor, we estimate potential sales of about $180,000 per year. We anticipate that half would come from school groups, with 25% from nature enthusiasts and 25% from casual nature strollers.

A second metric used in the industry is sales per square foot in the gift shop. Our industry research suggests $250 per square foot is attainable, which, with our 700 square foot gift shop, suggests potential annual sales of $175,000.

Finally, we estimate that within three years, one in eight visitors will purchase something from the gift shop, and will spend an average of $12.

7. What is it about your organization or your products that will make it likely that these customers will buy from you?

Our location adjacent to a major metropolitan area, with good highway access, our beautiful prairie ambiance, and the 120,000+ annual visitors to the nature center will help us attract customers.

8. For your target customers, who are the most likely primary competitors? (Summarize from Worksheet 5E.)

Our primary competitors include Riverview Nature Center gift shop, located on the other side of (and 30 miles farther away from) the metro area, two Discovery Channel stores in the metro area, and Birds of a Feather, a birding and bird feeding specialty store. While both offer quality products that might also interest our target customers, neither has our key advantages: a "destination" for 60,000 annual visitors, including 30,000 school and scout groups. However, given that these are our two primary competitors, we intend to closely monitor their pricing

(continued)

and product mix to make sure that we remain competitive and alert to emerging trends.

9. How will you make money from this venture?

It is typical in this industry to purchase products wholesale for approximately half of the retail price, resulting in a standard 100% markup. We'll make money from generating sufficient sales to cover all of our fixed costs (mostly staff) and earn a profit to benefit the nature center.

After enjoying a rewarding visit to the nature center, many people are looking for something to remember their visit, and are not in a bargain-hunting frame of mind. Also, visitors understand that their purchases help support the nature center.

Section III: The people

Tips for writing this section:

- The people section of the business plan is much more than a set of résumés. It details how the experience and expertise of the person in charge and the team make them best suited for success in this venture.

- Because assembling a good team is a key management step, the people section is best prepared by the person who will be running the business.

Worksheet 7D: The People on page 245 helps you assemble this section of your business plan. A sample follows.

Identify the people who will run this venture.

WORKSHEET 7D   The People

Instructions

❏ Answer the question below to identify the people who will manage the venture and
their responsibilities.

Example: **Nature center gift shop**

1. Who will be in charge of this venture activity? Why is he or she well-suited for this assignment? (Tie this to the needs of the venture—do not simply write "see attached résumé and job
   description.")

   > Jackie Olson will run the gift shop. Ms. Olson has ten years
   > of experience in nature-related gift shop retailing, including pri-
   > or work both in sales and retail management. Most important, she is
   > a skilled buyer of products that will appeal to this market, and has
   > demonstrated a good eye for designing or finding attractive yet inex-
   > pensive product displays. The feasibility study indicated that skills
   > in purchasing the right products and presenting them in an appealing
   > manner are two of the most important success factors for nature center
   > gift shops. Ms. Olson fits these two requirements well. She will work
   > on a 4/5's full-time basis.

   > Ms. Olson's résumé and the store manager's job description appear as an
   > attachment. The primary responsibilities of this position are person-
   > nel management, purchasing/inventory control, operations, product de-
   > velopment, marketing, and store merchandise/
   > display.

2. Who else will be on the management team carrying out the responsibilities of this venture?
   What skills do they have—tied in again to the needs of the venture—that will enable this to be
   a successful business?

   > An assistant manager will be hired on a half-time basis. That per-
   > son will be trained by the store manager to handle sales, restocking,
   > bookkeeping, and other duties as needed.

3. How will this activity be structured within the nonprofit? In other words, who will the person in
   charge of it report to? Where will the venture be situated in the organizational chart?

   > The store manager will report directly to the nature center executive
   > director.

(continued)

4. Who else inside and outside the organization will this venture work with to accomplish its goals?

> The store manager will work with other center staff including program planning, marketing, fundraising, and accounting. To develop products that match up with new programs, she will serve on the center program planning committee.
>
> She will work with center accounting staff to maintain appropriate business records, and be available to assist outside accountants during their annual audit. Occasional assistance from our outside law firm may be necessary to maintain compliance with tax and legal requirements.

Section IV: Implementation plans

The implementation section of the business plan contains four subsections. The *operational plan* describes the specific facilities, equipment, processes, and supply chains that will be used to produce and deliver products to the target market. The *marketing plan* describes what will be done to attract sufficient numbers of customers to purchase these products. The *start-up plan* describes steps to get the business ready to commence operations. And, finally, the *financial plan* presents multiyear financial projections of revenues, expenses, and cash flow for the proposed venture.

Operational plan

Tips for writing the operational plan:

- First, review Worksheet 5H: Operational Requirements. Those requirements typically concern five categories: facility, equipment, production processes, supply chain, and staffing. These requirements indicate what the venture needs in terms of operations.

- To complete this section, you show how you will meet those requirements. For example, facility requirements for a thrift store might include a busy thoroughfare, adjacent parking, adequate distance from the nearest competitor, minimum square footage, a loading dock, and signage authority. Therefore, the operational plan specifies the address of the proposed thrift shop, gives a description of the building, and explains how and why it meets the operational needs.

Worksheet 7E: Operational Plan on page 246 helps you write this section of the business plan. A sample follows.

Prepare the operational plan for this venture.

WORKSHEET 7E   Operational Plan

Instructions

❑ Pull out your Worksheet 5H: Operational Requirements.

❑ For each category, work out the details on how this venture will meet each requirement.

Example: **Nature center gift shop**

1. Facility. Where specifically will this venture be located? Are there other locations where work takes place? What improvements does the facility need? How does this location and the facility meet the requirements as stated in the feasibility study? What are the costs associated with acquiring and preparing this facility?

   The gift shop will be located adjacent to the entrance to the visitor center, in a space that contains 700 square feet of sales space. The space will be designed so visitors can enter the gift shop without having to pay the fee to enter the nature center. We have completed a floor plan study with expected locations of display fixtures and product categories. Adjacent to the shop there will be outdoor space for visitors to congregate, enjoy refreshments, and wait for naturalist tours to begin.

   As indicated in the feasibility study, product presentation is one of the key success factors in nature center gift shop retailing. The space layout, signage, fixtures, and product displays will support the store's theme.

   As a part of the center, the gift shop will use space provided to it by the center without having to pay rent. The gift shop will be responsible for outfitting the space with the necessary display fixtures and signage. As described in the floor plan study, the estimated cost for this is $11,000, which will be financed with a bank loan.

2. Equipment. What specific equipment or technology will be needed? How will this meet the equipment requirements? What will it cost to purchase and install this equipment?

   A point-of-sale computer system will be needed to track sales by product, price, and category. It will generate daily, weekly, monthly, and annual sales reports, which will then feed into our inventory tracking system so that reorders occur on a timely basis. Standard equipment for credit card validation will also be installed in the shop.

(continued)

We've been fortunate to receive a generous in-kind contribution from one of our board members, who is donating a used point-of-sale system from her business. She assures us that it will work fine for our needs for at least a few years.

A used desktop computer, monitor, modem, printer, and phone line will be provided by the center, so that gift shop staff can process orders from the web site, which will include a sample of popular products from the gift shop. Standard desktop and Internet access software will be utilized for this purpose.

3. Production Processes. How will the venture physically produce and deliver these products? How will this meet the process requirements? What costs are associated with these processes?

The gift shop will follow general processes common to the retail industry. On a daily basis, the three most important processes are sales transactions, handling cash, and inventory restocking. Success in the sales function requires hiring knowledgeable staff, training, and setting up procedures.

Procedures for handling cash will be established. We expect that most purchases will be made using credit cards or checks. No more than $200 in change will be kept in the cash register at any one time.

Costs for these processes are primarily staff and training costs, which are described in the financial plan section of this report and summarized in question 5 of this worksheet.

4. Supply Chain. How and from whom will this venture obtain the supplies it needs to be successful? How does this meet the supply chain requirements? What costs are expected from this?

We have identified and contacted six vendors who will provide 80% of the initial inventory required to open the gift shop. Expected initial orders from each vendor appear as an attachment. Each company appears to be in solid financial health (we ran a Dun & Bradstreet report on each of them), and has assured us of ample supply in all of our categories. As a result of the large initial orders we are contemplating, each vendor has agreed to offer us very favorable return policies for products that do not sell well.

The vendors will also grant us favorable financing terms, payable in thirty days, because our orders will be backed by the financial strength of the nature center.

(continued)

Worksheet 7E—Operational Plan

We are negotiating locally for assistance in designing and producing nature center image products, and have contacted several local artists whose work and pricing would be compatible with our needs in this area.

As indicated earlier, supply chain costs are primarily those from buying inventory at wholesale, where we expect to pay an average of 50% of our net sales price, and to pay freight, which is estimated at 2% of net sales price. Additional costs occur if nonreturnable inventory does not sell as expected or slower than expected, and for pilferage. We project that 1% of our inventory will fit into this category. The store manager will handle ordering.

5. Staffing. How will you meet the staffing requirements for this business? What do you anticipate your staffing costs will be?

In addition to the store manager, an assistant manager will be hired on a half full-time basis. He or she will be trained by the store manager to handle sales, restocking, bookkeeping, and other duties as needed.

The gift shop will be open an average of 45 hours per week. However, as we expect sales to be seasonal, hours will expand during our busy times (fall and spring migrations, spring flowers, early summer), and contract during quiet times (especially January and February).

We will utilize volunteers to help with restocking, inventory counts, and installing new displays. According to the Museum Store Association, 82% of nature museums use volunteers in their gift shops. Upon recommendation of other nature centers, we will only use paid staff to handle sales transactions, with volunteers to help with a variety of other functions. The nature center has a large pool of volunteers, and a number have already expressed interest in helping out with the gift shop, knowing that it will help support the nature center. We will also offer work-study internships for local students seeking experience in this field.

Our projections suggest that, by the third year, staffing the gift shop will cost about $50,000 per year, including fringe benefits. This works out to be about 32% of projected net sales, which fits in well with industry standards.

Marketing plan

Tips for writing the marketing plan:

- First, review Worksheet 5G: Marketing Requirements. These requirements indicate what the venture needs in terms of marketing to attract its target customers.

- To prepare your marketing plan, you will need to decide on the actions management will take to fulfill those marketing requirements.

- You don't need to be a marketing expert to prepare your marketing plan. However, you do need an understanding of who your target customers are (Worksheet 5B), which of their wants and needs you propose to meet (Worksheets 5C and 5D), and what they currently purchase (or do) to meet those wants and needs (Worksheets 5E and 5F). So, while working on your marketing plan, study the worksheets from Step 5 carefully. Discuss them with your venture team and entrepreneurial committee to get their marketing suggestions.

- Defining your position in the market is often the first step in marketing. Positioning is essentially how you would like your customers to distinguish your venture in their mind.[24] Your marketing efforts should be designed to help establish and reinforce that impression. A question on positioning appears in Worksheet 7F.

- Remember that successful marketing involves a mixture of *research* and *communication*. The research and analysis has to be done so you'll have a good handle on what kinds of communications will be effective. Communications often involve expensive promotions such as direct mail, advertisements, and brochures. It's also worth recalling, however, that mentioning the venture in virtually every newsletter, brochure, press release, speech, web site, and so on that the nonprofit puts out can have an even bigger impact. It is often true in marketing that the most effective communication efforts are simple and inexpensive.

Worksheet 7F: Marketing Plan, page 248, helps you write the marketing portion of your business plan. A sample follows.

Prepare the marketing plan for this venture.

Start-up plan

Tips for writing the start-up plan:

- Select a target date for the venture to open its doors for business. Write down everything you can think of that has to be ready by then.

- For each item on that list, work backwards in time to determine the lead time for that item to be in place on opening day. Indicate who will be responsible for doing it or making sure it gets done.

Worksheet 7G: Start-up Plan, page 250, helps you write the start-up portion of your business plan. A sample is on page 147.

Prepare the start-up plan for this venture.

WORKSHEET 7F   Marketing Plan

Instructions

❑ Review Worksheet 5G: Marketing Requirements.

❑ Make decisions on your marketing strategies.

Example: **Nature center gift shop**

1. What are the marketing goals for this venture?

> **In general, the gift shop's primary goals are twofold: (1) to get nature center visitors to enter the store and (2) to get visitors who enter the store to become customers. Everything we do is directed towards accomplishing these two goals.**
>
> **We have the following specific goals to achieve by the third year of the store's operation:**
>
> **- one in every eight visitors will become a customer**
>
> **- each customer will spend an average of $12 in the store**
>
> **Assuming the nature center continues to attract at least 120,000 visitors per year, that equals net sales of $180,000 per year.**

2. What are the key marketing requirements to succeed in attracting target customers? (Lift this answer from question 7 of Worksheet 5G.)

> **We organized the marketing requirements into three categories: product selection, presentation, and communication. Facility issues are discussed under operational requirements.**
>
> **Product selection**
>
> **- Products must fit with the values of the nature center, but must also appeal to our customers and sell quickly.**
>
> **- Products must appeal to children. Store manager will need to keep current on changing tastes, from dinosaurs one year to astronauts the next.**
>
> **- Weekly tracking of sales by product to highlight and reorder fast-selling merchandise, and remove slow-moving stock.**

(continued)

<u>Presentation</u>

- Attractive, highly visible signage that pulls park visitors into the gift shop. Placement of attractive items at gift shop entrance that catch the attention of each customer segment.

- Placement of toy bins at young kid level (i.e., 18 inches above the floor) near the shop entrance to attract children and provide them the opportunity to "touch and feel" objects before purchasing them.

- Style uniformity for all signage and print materials, so they are consistent in font, color, logo use, and so on. Examples include brochures, shopping bags, and web site.

<u>Communication</u>

- Mechanism in place to do frequent surveys of visitors and customers to identify their interests and impressions.

- Coordinate with nature center staff to leverage communication efforts. For example, starting and ending naturalist tours at the gift shop, holding special events in the store (such as lectures, readings, how-to demonstrations), and mentioning the gift shop in brochures, newsletters, and press releases.

- Reminders that all purchases help support the nature center.

- Collect customer names, addresses, and purchases for gift shop's database. Regular mailings about special events in the store (such as readings or how-to demonstrations) and sales.

3. How will this venture be positioned relative to your competitors? How will you price your products, and how will that compare to your competitors' pricing?

Our overall positioning strategy is to be known as *the trusted* place to go for nature-inspired merchandise. For center visitors, we will be the only place in town to get souvenirs of their visit.

We will price our products competitively with other stores that sell like items. We do not expect that our customers will be able to find our products locally at lower prices. Some products may be available cheaper on the Internet, but we are not concerned given the spontaneity that accompanies purchasing from a gift shop.

(continued)

4. What communication strategies will be undertaken to satisfy the marketing requirements and your positioning statement? What is the timetable for these activities? What strategies will focus on getting repeat business from existing customers as opposed to attracting new customers?

Rate of sale will be tested through small initial orders and then reordering those items that sell well. Keeping prices low will be important to maintain a quick rate of turnover.

A merchandise mix study was done to determine the nature of the products for each product category, and the square footage and expected inventory value by category. We have also completed a floor plan study that shows locations of display fixtures and product categories.

Strategies targeted at each of our customer segments are as follows:

- <u>Nature enthusiasts</u>: The gift shop will coordinate with the center's marketing efforts, "tagging along" with promotions intended to bring people to the center and special activities. Appealing signage will be placed near the shop to entice visitors inside to browse and then purchase.

- <u>Nature center members</u>, who are a subgroup of this segment, will receive information via a quarterly newsletter, which the gift shop will use to highlight items that relate to the current exhibition or advertise special events such as seasonal sales. Additionally, several times each year we will send postcard-sized promotions, usually connected with a specific activity. Finally, members (as well as volunteers, board, and staff) will receive a 10% discount on their purchases.

- <u>Casual nature strollers</u>: The window display will feature dynamic themes that have a high visual impact. Attractive displays will encourage buying gifts especially during the holiday season. All naturalist tours will begin and end in front of the gift shop.

- <u>School and scout groups</u>: Our informal focus groups with school and scout leaders have identified the types of products they would be interested in seeing in the store. Special packages will be created with $2 and $5 assortments to enable school and scout leaders to save them time (and hassle) by making one purchase for their group.

(continued)

Several strategies will be used to encourage repeat business. We will have a "frequent shoppers club" that gives a 20% discount on next purchase after $200 worth of merchandise has been purchased. A mailing list will be developed of customers who are not nature center members and they will be mailed a card similar to the one mailed to members several times per year. To keep costs down, we will use the same artwork with a different message on the back. Names for the mailing list will be taken from frequent shoppers club and customers will be encouraged to add their names to our mailing list to receive special notices and discounts when paying for items.

5. What will it cost to carry out these activities? What's the timeline for these efforts?

As part of the nature center, we will be able to draw upon internal resources, so our out-of-pocket marketing costs will be minimal for marketing. We've budgeted $3000 per year for such out-of-pocket expenses.

Here's the timeline for the most significant initial promotional efforts:

- July-August: work with nature center staff to incorporate gift shop in most if not all brochures, press releases, web site, etc. Begin planning for grand opening.

- September: schedule special events in the gift shop to start October 1 (readings, lectures, how-to demonstrations)

- October: advertise in local community paper about OctoberFest specials on sale at the gift shop

6. Who will evaluate the effectiveness of these marketing efforts? How and when will they do so?

The store manager will have responsibility for measuring results of the various marketing efforts. To do that, we will continuously collect data on purchasing patterns, and compare that against our marketing efforts.

Records will be kept of customer comments and product requests. Staff will also be trained to keep informal tabs on which kinds of items are being purchased by which customer segment.

WORKSHEET 7G   Start-up Plan

Instructions

❑ Decide on a target start date for the business

❑ Write down what needs to be completed by the date. For help, refer back to
Worksheet 7E: Operational Plan and 7F: Marketing Plan.

❑ For each item on your list, determine how much lead time is required, how it
will be done, and who will be responsible for completing it. Keep in mind that
some items need to be completed before work on other items can begin.

Example: **Nature center gift shop**

1. What is the target date for the business to commence operations? How fixed is that date—
what are the consequences if the start is delayed?

> **The gift shop will open for business on October 1, 2002. This date is
> fixed: we have to be open for the fall bird migration season, which is
> one of our most popular times for visitors. It would be a major missed
> opportunity if the gift shop were to open any later than this.**

2. What are the key tasks that need to be completed in order to launch the business on the
target date? What is the timeline for each task? How will each part get done—and by whom?
Refer to your operational (Worksheet 7E) and marketing (Worksheet 7F) plans.

> - **Financing.** In May, the executive director and store manager will
>   present bank with business plan and financing request.
>   A formal approval decision has been promised within two weeks. In-
>   formally, bank manager indicated that, with our proposed collateral,
>   approval is expected.
>
> - **Staffing.** On July 1, store manager will be hired as a permanent staff
>   member. She currently works for the nature center on a contract ba-
>   sis. She will hire an assistant manager by August 1, and provide
>   sales training during August. Volunteers will be interviewed and se-
>   lected in August and trained in September.
>
> - **Facility.** In June, facilities staff will clear the indoor space and
>   install new lighting. In July, facilities staff will oversee con-
>   struction of the outdoor visitor space adjacent to the gift shop.
>   Also in July, facilities staff will install fixtures and furniture.
>   In September, signage will be selected and prepared.

(continued)

- <u>Equipment.</u> In August, once the fixtures and furniture have been installed, store manager will arrange for installation and testing of point-of-sale computer system

- <u>Supply chain.</u> In June, store manager will select and order initial inventory for the gift shop. In July and August, as inventory arrives and after fixtures and furniture have been installed, she and facilities staff will create, design, and construct displays for the opening.

- <u>Processes.</u> In July, store manager will create a procedure manual for handling sales, restocking and reordering inventory, and accounting.

- <u>Marketing.</u> Starting in July, store manager will work with the communications director to promote and incorporate the gift shop in the nature center's newsletter, mailings, press releases, and web site. For example, the nature center expects to receive a fair amount of publicity in connection with the October opening of the new wetland bird watching boardwalk. We will piggyback on that publicity by bringing reporters through the gift shop, and pointing out books and equipment there that will enable visitors to better appreciate wetland bird watching.

	APR	MAY	JUN	JUL	AUG	SEP	OCT
Secure bank financing		■					
Clear indoor space			■				
Install fixtures & furniture				■			
Install pt-of-sale system					■		
Construct product displays					■		
Prepare, install signage						■	
Order initial inventory			■				
Receive & log inventory				■	■		
Place product on displays						■	

Store Grand Opening Oct. 1

Financial plan

Tips for writing the financial plan:

- Pull out Worksheet 6C: Financial Projections and Summary from the feasibility study. Make corrections and changes as needed to reflect the decisions you have made since you began work on the business plan. Staffing, operations, and marketing costs should be considerably clearer now, and those clarifications need to be reflected in the financial projections.

- Be sure to include a detailed set of notes of your assumptions and the calculations used for the financial projections.

- Every financial plan needs to have annual income statements and cash flow summaries for the first three years of operations. Also, monthly detailed cash flow statements should be prepared for the first year. Finally, a sources and uses of financing statement is appropriate for ventures that will require financing.

Financing your venture. A business plan identifies the start-up costs that will be incurred before the business is able to pay its own way. These costs include such things as equipment, inventory, space, marketing, and staffing. Finding the means to finance these costs is often a major problem for nonprofits contemplating venture development.

In rare instances, grants or gifts are available to cover start-up costs. However, in most cases, nonprofits use some of their own funds for this purpose, often supplemented with money they borrow from outside the organization. Internal resources, which vary depending on the organization, are the first place to look for start-up funds.

- *Internal sources.* Internal sources include operating reserves, discretionary funds, and flexible grants where such spending is appropriate. Some organizations decide venture development is a good time to redirect internal resources currently targeted for an existing activity that is not as close to their mission or strategic objectives as the proposed venture. Board members sometimes provide start-up funds in the form of gifts or low-interest loans, and in some cases senior staff or members of the entrepreneurial committee do the same.

  There are two reasons to consider internal sources before pursuing outside financing. First, these funds are generally easier to gain access to—typically upon staff recommendation and board approval. Second, external financing sources often insist that the nonprofit demonstrate its commitment to the venture by putting some of its own money at risk. When you finally meet with external sources, you will be able to indicate the level of internal resources (including in-kind contributions such as staff time and space) that the nonprofit is planning to invest in the venture.

- *Traditional financing.* After exhausting internal sources, the next area to consider is traditional financing. The most common source of financing for ventures are loans from banks, which are, after all, in the business of lending money to help businesses grow. But don't expect it to be easy to get start-up financing this way. Bankers are generally wary of new ventures (they prefer ongoing businesses with an established track record of sales and profits), and they often show even less enthusiasm for ventures started up by nonprofits.

  The best bet is to work with the bank where your organization has an established banking relationship, presumably at least a checking and savings account. Because of that relationship, your bank has an added incentive to consider doing more business with you. Your bank knows that if you find a loan at another bank, that bank will probably ask you to move your accounts there as well. While bankers will want to see your business plan and review the evidence that you can succeed with this business, typically they will require collateral to secure the loan as well. Often nonprofits will use internal reserves or equity in a building as collateral.

- *Venture philanthropy.* A nontraditional source of outside financing is known as venture philanthropy, where foundations and well-to-do individuals provide low- or no-interest loans. While this may sound like manna from heaven, and sometimes it is, in practice these dollars are scarce and narrowly focused. Program-related investments (PRIs), where below-market loans are provided for projects deemed to have important social or community benefits, are in this category.[25]

- *Strategic partners.* Another possibility for financing a venture is to form a strategic partnership, where two (or more) organizations craft an agreement to work together on a business venture. The typical arrangement is for a nonprofit to link up with a for-profit company, although strategic venture partnerships between nonprofits are now becoming more common. Frequently the for-profit provides most of the start-up financing, with the nonprofit contributing name recognition, staff expertise, and so on. Proceeds are usually distributed in some fashion in proportion to the value (to the venture) of the investment each party makes.

Sources and Uses of Financing. The sources-and-uses statement identifies the financing this venture will need to start and operate for its first three years (uses), and where the nonprofit intends to secure that financing (sources). Uses include equipment, inventory, and working capital. Working capital refers to funds needed to cover operating costs until the business becomes profitable. This is calculated from the cash flow statements. If your projections indicate cash flow deficits—which commonly occur during the first year or two of most ventures—additional working capital will be needed so that the venture can continue to pay its bills.

It's important to include internal contributions as well on the sources-and-uses statement. To demonstrate commitment, nonprofits often indicate grants and in-kind contributions they expect to receive in conjunction with starting this business.

Following is an example of a sources-and-uses-of-financing statement.

	Build-Out Space & Displays	Initial Inventory	Working Capital	Financing Totals
Reserves	$0	$0	$7,000	$7,000
Bank loan(5 years @ 8%)	$11,000	$19,000	$15,000	$45,000
In-kind (labor)	$ 10,000	$0	$0	$ 10,000
Uses Totals	$21,000	$19,000	$22,000	$62,000

You crunched most of the numbers you will need for the financial plan during Step 6. Worksheet 7H: Financial Plan on page 251 helps you gather in one place all those numbers. An example for this worksheet does not follow. Instead, to see the complete financial plan for the nature center gift shop, turn to Appendix D: Sample Financial Plan for Nature Center Gift Shop on page 173.

Prepare the financial plan for this business.

Section V: Contingencies

Tips for completing this section:

- As the last section of the business plan (prior to the appendix), contingencies is the place to lay out the risks and uncertainties that exist in every business plan. It's basically the "what if" section of the plan. What if sales run lower than expectations? What if our competitors lower their prices and we're forced to match them to remain competitive? If it turns out this is *not* a great venture idea after all, how difficult (and expensive) will it be for us to quit this venture? It's best to identify these issues early and start thinking up ways to respond.

Many of the contingencies draw on the risks you identified in Step 6. Worksheet 7I: Contingencies on page 252 helps you review those uncertainties and plan for responses. A sample is on page 152.

Identify the contingencies for this business.

WORKSHEET 7I   Contingencies

Instructions

❑ Pull out Worksheet 6D: Risks.

❑ For each of the key risks identified in that worksheet, describe how you will minimize the chance of the event occurring, or how you would respond if it were to occur.

Example: **Nature center gift shop**

1. What are the most serious risks that were identified in Worksheet 6D? Are there any other serious risks that you have become aware of since doing that worksheet?

   Risk is that sales will not reach projected levels, either because visitor numbers go down, or we don't do as good a job of pulling them into the shop to become customers.

2. Why do you believe these risks are not so worrisome that the business should not be started?

   We are confident that we can achieve or exceed our projections. All the evidence we have gathered from our customers and from other nature center gift shops supports our confidence.

3. What will you do to minimize the likelihood that these risks will be realized and create a problem for the business?

   We've designed an aggressive marketing plan, the results from which we will continuously monitor and adjust over time.

4. If these risks do occur, what steps will you take to prevent them from harming the business?

   We would make changes to our marketing strategies. We would bring in an external gift shop marketing consultant to advise on the steps we need to take. If necessary, we would limit the hours the store is open to those that bring the largest number of visitors, reducing staffing costs accordingly.

Supporting documents

Most business plans end with an appendix containing documents that support the rest of the plan. These might include

- Notes to financial statements
- Equipment list
- Site plan
- Résumés of management and key staff
- Insurance requirements and costs
- Regulatory issues

Get the plan approved

The assumption at the beginning of this step was that your entrepreneurial committee and your board had approved the feasibility study (Steps 5 and 6), which is to say they agreed that the venture was feasible and asked for preparation of a business plan to launch it. If the financials and risks of the feasibility study have not changed significantly for the business plan, then upon approval by senior management, it's time to launch the business. If there have been major changes to the financial statements and risks, or if the feasibility study was incomplete in either of these areas, then it makes sense to get entrepreneurial committee approval first, followed by the board's approval.

Circulate the completed Step 7 worksheets to your venture team. Present the business plan to whoever needs to approve it.

Step 7 summary

The business plan is essentially a structured exercise to clarify and present the central issues that will determine the success of your new venture. A good business plan provides the information your audience needs to understand why this venture will succeed, and how you will get it started. As the venture grows, the business plan provides a framework to evaluate it.

Chapter Four Summary

Congratulations! You are about to give birth to a new venture. By completing the worksheets in this chapter, you now know what to do to turn this idea into a successful, operating business. After all the work gathering information, making decisions, and filling out worksheets, you're probably both excited and worried—excited that you can stop studying and start running the venture; worried after looking at the risks and uncertainties. The truth of the matter is that almost every entrepreneur has some lingering concerns before taking the plunge. That's healthy. There are no guarantees in the business world, so it's best to be aware of the problems as well as the opportunities as you turn planning into action.

You've probably discovered from your research that your venture has more than a few unexpected requirements, uncertainties, and competitors. But rest assured. If you've followed the steps in this book, and obtained reviews of your work by your venture team, your entrepreneurial committee, and your board, you've been prudent and cautious given the uncertainties of entrepreneurship. You are ready to start the business.

This is a good time to recall why your organization decided to pursue ventures in the first place. For most nonprofits, ventures are not just about making money, but also about making mission—to do more good for the people they serve, for the causes they care about. The venture you are about to launch is intended to do just that. Getting to this point has taken a great deal of work, work that has been worthwhile because it will help your organization do more good.

Now it's your turn—to get your business started. Go for it.

 Start the business.

Good luck!

Conclusion

Here are a few things to keep in mind as you implement the business plan and begin operating your venture.

Focus on the Basics

Most businesses operate with a simple, core business concept. In a nutshell, a venture needs to sell customers what they want, at a price they feel is fair, with enough left over to meet profit requirements. For almost every business, managers need to work on four things simultaneously: increase sales, manage cash flow, achieve margins, and control expenses. Each is important and none can be accomplished at the expense of another.

Many nonprofit ventures also operate with a social as well as a financial bottom line, which becomes a key part of the mix. As with most things, the trick is how to manage the details—where to put energy and resources to accomplish your targets. That's why finding the right management team is so critical.

Find the Right Venture Champions

A champion is someone who has a strong personal commitment to the success of the venture. The person who manages the venture needs to be a venture champion. It is impossible to overstate the importance of finding the right person to run the business. While the research and business planning effort is a necessary component of success, it is not sufficient without a suitably trained, motivated individual committed to success.

In the private sector, this role is often filled by the business owner, who has invested significant personal funds and unpaid time, and is motivated by the potential to achieve personal wealth from the venture. This is the kind of person who puts in sixty-hour weeks, and then wakes up at 3 A.M. to jot down an idea on how to solve a nagging business problem. While nonprofit ventures do not have "owners" in the same way, success in these ventures is much more likely if they are managed by someone with a similar sense of personal ownership.

The venture manager is not the only person who has a personal stake in the business. Another champion for the venture is often the person who handles the financial, quantitative side of the business. In small start-ups, the venture manager sometimes does both jobs, but as the venture grows that function should be delegated to someone who fully understands and supports the purpose and goals of the business. Many successful nonprofit ventures use a team approach at the top. The top person is the visionary, risk-seeking entrepreneur, and just below him or her on the organizational chart is the finance-numbers person to ground those visions in practicality.

It takes a champion

"We knew that our training programs were exceptional, but our staff only wanted to provide them for free to needy people. For years, we had limited success getting our staff to sell our programs to customers who could pay for them. At one point, we were ready to stop trying to sell the program, as meager sales just weren't worth the impact on staff morale. Then, at the last minute, we found the right person—an ambidextrous entrepreneur who understood in her heart and soul that making money was worthwhile because doing so would allow us to serve more needy people. With this champion on board, the whole culture of our organization began to shift, over time, to an attitude of prosperity rather than poverty. As a result of this shift, our programs and services are thriving, we are earning more money than ever before, and donations have actually increased because we're so popular. We are now doing a better job of doing our mission, serving more needy people than we ever did before. But it took a huge culture shift—driven by the right person—to make our ventures work."[26]

Review Marketing Strategies Often

Many nonprofit ventures face their first "surprise" when initial sales turn out lower than expected. The marketing effort may not have been as aggressive as envisioned, or perhaps the growth projections were unrealistic. Whatever the cause, your marketing plan should be continually evaluated and retooled based on your experiences attracting customers. Create systems to track how customers found out about your business, why they decided to buy from you, and how they felt about the product or service you provided. If you can, talk to prospective customers who decided not to buy from you. Finally, keep track of how your competitors are promoting themselves, and don't be reluctant to imitate them if what they're doing is working.

Measure Performance Quantitatively

Most ventures track sales, gross margin, and operating and sales expenses, each as a percent of sales, along with cash flow. Your research in operational requirements (Step 5) probably uncovered several other key performance ratios that are associated with success in this business. Each performance number should be calculated, and compared against the business plan and the previous year's results, on a monthly basis. The venture manager will need to be able to explain the causes underlying major variances, and whether a negative variance represents a potential problem for the venture that needs to be addressed or is simply a matter of timing.

Get Outside Help

Every venture should establish some kind of a formal or informal advisory committee to provide outside perspective and advice. In many cases, members of your entrepreneurial committee will be interested in continuing to help with the idea they worked on as it evolves into an ongoing business. As with the entrepreneurial committee, it's a good idea to invite at least two members of the nonprofit's board of directors to serve on this committee as well. Of course, if you've decided to create a separate organization to run the venture, then it will have its own board to oversee the business. Consultants can provide expertise and direction, particularly to make changes if the business is not meeting its goals and there is a need to evaluate options and opportunities.

Compare Your Plan with Reality

Your business plan should be seen as a living document that changes as you learn more about the business from operating it. On at least an annual basis, you should review the budgets and conclusions from your business plan and revise them accordingly. Which of your start-up assumptions proved to be incorrect? Which of these are environmental factors, in the sense that you can do little to change them? Which can you do something about?

Every business encounters disappointment at one point or another. Sales do not meet expectations, costs are higher than anticipated, or fierce competition emerges from an unforeseen direction. The hallmarks of a successful entrepreneur are persistence and creativity; these qualities enable the entrepreneur to see through barriers to the opportunities that lie on the other side, and then to take effective action to get there.

Notes

1. Personal correspondence February 2001.

2. Independent Sector web site, 2001. Private payments, defined as "primarily dues, fees and charges," as a percent of budget, by sector: arts and culture, 24 percent; social and legal, 19 percent; education/research, 56 percent; health services, 48 percent. 1996 data.

3. Example contributed by Karen Simmons, director, La Salle University Nonprofit Center. Used with permission.

4. Example used with permission from Saint Paul Neighborhood Consortium. From a consulting meeting with Rolfe Larson Associates.

5. Example used with permission from Dharma Enterprises. From a project of Rolfe Larson Associates.

6. *Fast Company*, January-February 2000, vol. 31, p. 81.

7. *Cosmic Religion*, New York: Covici-Friedo, 1931. Thanks to the Albert Einstein Archives, The Hebrew University of Jerusalem, Israel.

8. Discussion on project leader and venture team responsibilities adapted with permission from consulting materials developed by The National Center for Social Entrepreneurs.

9. Example contributed by Karen Simmons, director, La Salle University Nonprofit Center. Used with permission.

10. Example used with permission from Breakthrough Urban Ministries. From a project author worked on with The National Center for Social Entrepreneurs.

11. Discussion and worksheet on core competencies adapted with permission from The National Center for Social Entrepreneurs consulting materials.

12. Example used with permission from Ohio Hunger Task Force. From a project author worked on with The National Center for Social Entrepreneurs.

13. Discussion on entrepreneurial committee adapted with permission from The National Center for Social Entrepreneurs consulting materials.

14. Example in Worksheet 4A and 4B used with permission from Provident Counseling. From a project author worked on with The National Center for Social Entrepreneurs.

15. Examples used with permission from each nonprofit. From projects author worked on with The National Center for Social Entrepreneurs.

16. Worksheet adapted with permission from The National Center for Social Entrepreneurs consulting materials.

17. A valuable resource about focus groups is Judith Sharken Simon's book *The Nonprofit Field Guide to Conducting Successful Focus Groups*, published by Fieldstone Alliance.

18. Example used with permission from Brody•Weiser•Burns, a consulting firm located in Branford, CT.

19. Discussion and worksheet on success factors adapted with permission from The National Center for Social Entrepreneurs consulting materials.

20. For more information about competitive advantage and strategy, see Michael Porter, *Competitive Strategy*.

21. Worksheet on competitive advantage adapted with permission from The National Center for Social Entrepreneurs consulting materials.

22. Two sources of additional information on marketing are Gary Stern's book *Marketing Workbook for Nonprofit Organizations Volume I: Develop the Plan, 2nd Edition*, published Fieldstone Alliance, 2001, and Harry Beckwith's *Selling the Invisible,* published by Warner Books, 1997.

23. See Harry Beckwith, *Selling the Invisible*.

24. A guide to positioning your product or service is included in Gary Stern's book *Marketing Workbook for Nonprofit Organizations Volume I.*

25. A report summarizing concepts and opportunities in this area is the Marino Institute's publication: *Venture Philanthropy 2001: The Changing Landscape*, published by The Marino Institute, 2001. Free download available at www.marino.org.

26. Case example contributed by Karen Simmons, director, La Salle University Nonprofit Center. Used with permission.

Appendices

Appendix A
Bibliography

Alter, Sutia Kim. *Managing the Double Bottom Line: A Business Planning Guide for Social Enterprise*. Washington, DC: Save the Children Federation, 2000.

Beckwith, Harry. *Selling the Invisible: A Field Guide to Modern Marketing*. New York, NY: Warner Books, 1997.

Boschee, Jerr. *The Social Enterprise Sourcebook: Profiles of Social Purpose Businesses Operated by Nonprofit Organizations*. Minneapolis, MN: Northland Institute, 2001.

Brinckerhoff, Peter C. *Social Entrepreneurship: The Art of Mission-Based Venture Development*. New York, NY: John Wiley & Sons, 2000.

Brown, Peter C. *The Complete Guide to Money-Making Ventures for Nonprofit Organizations*. Detroit, MI: The Taft Group, 1986.

Cohen, Ben, et al. *Ben & Jerry's Double-Dip: How to Run a Values-Led Business and Make Money, Too*. New York, NY: Simon & Schuster, 1997.

Collins, James C., and Jerry Porras. *Built to Last: Successful Habits of Visionary Companies*. New York, NY: HarperBusiness, 1994.

Dees, J. Gregory, Jed Emerson, and Peter Economy. *Enterprising Nonprofits: A Toolkit for Social Entrepreneurs*. New York: John Wiley & Sons, 2001.

Emerson, Jed, and Fay Twersky. *New Social Entrepreneurs: The Success, Challenge, and Lessons of Non-Profit Enterprise Creation*. San Francisco, CA: The Roberts Foundation, 1996.

Espy, Siri N. *Marketing Strategies for Nonprofit Organizations*. Chicago, IL: Lyceum Books, 1993.

Firstenberg, Paul B. *Managing for Profit in the Nonprofit World*. New York, NY: The Foundation Center, 1988.

———. *The 21st Century Nonprofit: Remaking the Organization in the Post-Government Era*. New York, NY: The Foundation Center, 1996.

Godin, Seth. *Permission Marketing: Turning Strangers into Friends, and Friends into Customers*. New York, NY: Simon & Schuster, 1999.

Grobman, Gary M. *The Nonprofit Organization's Guide to E-Commerce*. Harrisburg, PA: White Hat Communications, 2000.

Hopkins, Bruce R. *Starting and Managing a Nonprofit Organization: A Legal Guide, Third Edition*. New York, NY: John Wiley & Sons, 2001.

Kotler, Philip, and Alan R. Andreasen. *Strategic Marketing for Nonprofit Organizations, Fifth Edition*. Upper Saddle River, NJ: Prentice Hall, 1996.

Landy, Laura. *Something Ventured, Something Gained: A Business Development Guide for Nonprofit Organizations*. New York, NY: ACA Books, 1989.

Lukas, Carol A. *Consulting with Nonprofits: A Practitioner's Guide*. Saint Paul, MN: Fieldstone Alliance, 1998.

Maitland, Arnaud. *Masterwork: Master of Time*. Berkeley, CA: Dharma Publishing, 2000.

Mingo, Jack. *How the Cadillac Got Its Fins: And Other Tales from the Annals of Business and Marketing*. New York, NY: HarperBusiness, 1994.

Morino Institute. V*enture Philanthropy 2001: The Changing Landscape*. Reston, VA: Morino Institute, 2001. (download from www.morino.org)

Porter, Michael E. *Competitive Strategy: Techniques for Analyzing Industries and Competitors*. New York, NY: Free Press, 1980.

Ries, Al, and Jack Trout. *The 22 Immutable Laws of Marketing*. New York, NY: HarperCollins, 1993.

Robert, Michel. *Product Innovation Strategy Pure and Simple*. New York, NY: McGraw Hill, 1995.

Sealy, Kelvin, Jerr Boschee, Jed Emerson, and Wendy Sealey. *A Reader in Social Enterprise*. Boston, MA: Pearson Custom Publishers, 2000.

Sharken Simon, Judith. *The Wilder Nonprofit Field Guide to Conducting Successful Focus Groups*. Saint Paul, MN: Fieldstone Alliance, 1999.

Shore, Bill. *Revolution of the Heart: A New Strategy for Creating Wealth and Meaningful Change*. New York, NY: Berkeley Publishing, 1995.

———. *The Cathedral Within: Transforming Your Life by Giving Something Back*. New York, NY: Random House, 1999.

Skloot, Edward. *The Nonprofit Entrepreneur: Creating Ventures to Earn Income*. New York, NY: The Foundation Center, 1988.

Steckel, Richard, Robin Simons, Peter Lengsfelder, and Jennifer Lahman. *Filthy Rich: How to Turn Your Nonprofit Fantasies info Cold, Hard Cash*. Berkeley, CA: Ten Speed Press, 2000.

Steckel, Richard, Robin Simons, Jeffrey Simons, and Norman Tanen. *Making Money While Making a Difference: How to Profit with a Nonprofit Partner*. Homewood, IL: High Tide Press, 1999.

Stern, Gary. *Marketing Workbook for Nonprofit Organizations, Volume I: Develop the Plan, 2nd Edition*. Saint Paul, MN: Fieldstone Alliance, 2001.

———. *Marketing Workbook for Nonprofit Organizations, Volume II: Mobilize People for Marketing Success*. Saint Paul, MN: Fieldstone Alliance, 1997.

Appendix B
Internet Resources

www.ashoka.org

Ashoka: Innovators for the Public is a nonprofit that offers financial and professional support to social entrepreneurs around the world.

www.brodyweiser.com

Brody•Weiser•Burns is a management consulting firm with a mission to help focus and strengthen the efforts of organizations working toward progressive social change.

www.communitywealth.org

Community Wealth Ventures, Inc., is a for-profit enterprise that delivers strategic counsel to corporations, foundations, and nonprofit organizations interested in creating community wealth.

www.echoinggreen.org

The Echoing Green Foundation provides full-time fellowships to emerging social entrepreneurs in the United States and internationally.

www.egroups.com/invite/nonprofit_entrepreneurship

This is an online discussion group about nonprofit entrepreneurship.

www.entreworld.org

Entreworld is a project of the Kauffman Center for Entrepreneurial Leadership that includes publications and links on entrepreneurship.

www.genie.org

The California Management Assistance Partnership's web site includes information and resources for the nonprofit community.

www.independentsector.org

Independent Sector is a trade association for nonprofit organizations; its web site includes information about creating partnerships with the private sector.

www.irs.gov

The Internal Revenue Service's web site offers information on tax issues for nonprofit organizations. See especially Publication 598, *Tax on Unrelated Business Income of Exempt Organizations.*

www.morino.org

The Morino Institute has a special interest in venture philanthropy as an approach to bringing resources to the nonprofit sector.

www.managementhelp.org

Management Help is a free downloadable library on a large number of management topics for nonprofit organizations including social entrepreneurship.

www.nationalgathering.org

The National Gathering for Social Entrepreneurs is exclusively devoted to providing support for social entrepreneurs. They have an annual conference that provides training and networking for both novice and experienced managers in this field.

www.onlinewbc.gov

The Small Business Administration's Online Women's Business Center exists to "level the playing field" for women entrepreneurs and offers resources and programs to help women start and build successful businesses.

www.redf.org

The Roberts Enterprise Development Fund supports social-purpose ventures as a means to expand economic opportunity for homeless and very low-income individuals. Its web site includes publications on social return on investment and on managing social purpose enterprises.

www.rolfelarson.com

Rolfe Larson Associates is a marketing, finance, and venture consulting firm that helps social entrepreneurs and small businesses develop new ventures and expand existing ones.

www.sba.gov

The Small Business Administration offers information and resources on starting and financing a small business.

www.socialentrepreneurs.org

The National Center for Social Entrepreneurs is a nonprofit consulting firm that helps organizations become more effective and financially self-sufficient.

www.fieldstonealliance.org

Fieldstone Alliance offers practical guides to help nonprofit managers accomplish their mission.

Appendix C
Internet Research Links

Search engines

AltaVista altavista.com - large; advanced search features.

Dogpile dogpile.com - searches multiple search engines.

Excite excite.com - concept searching.

Google google.com - large and comprehensive

Hotbot hotbot.com - unique sorting capabilities.

Lycos lycos.com - specialty search resources.

Northern Light northernlight.com - creates custom search folders.

Subject guides

Yahoo! yahoo.com

About about.com

Newspapers, periodicals, and related web sites

American City Business Journals bizjournals.bcentral.com

Business Week www.businessweek.com

Fast Company www.fastcompany.com

Inc Online www.inc.com

Listserv List Reference www.lsoft.com/lists/listref.html

Newsbot (news service) www.newsbot.com

Newspage (industry news) www.newspage.com.sg

Nonprofit Times www.nptimes.com

Virtual Reference Desk www.refdesk.com/paper.html

Wall Street Journal www.wsj.com

Washington Post www.washingtonpost.com

Wired www.wired.com

Government

Bureau of the Census www.census.gov

Consumer Information Center www.pueblo.gsa.gov

Index of state & local government www.loc.gov/global/state

Internal Revenue Service www.irs.gov

Library of Congress card catalog www.loc.gov/catalog

Securities and Exchange Commission's business database www.sec.gov/edgar.shtml

Private

Directory of Publishers and VendorsAssociations and Institutes www.library.vanderbilt.edu/acqweb/pubr/asso.html

Dun & Bradstreet www.dnb.com

Phone, address & e-mail lookup service people.yahoo.com

Small Business Advisor www.isquare.com (links & resources by state)

Private databases (available at many libraries)

ABI Inform CD-ROM (citations/abstracts from business and management periodicals)

Business Dateline CD-ROM (full-text articles from hundreds of regional publications)

Wall Street Journal Ondisc, New York Times Ondisc

Appendix D

Sample Financial Plan
for Nature Center Gift Shop

Three-Year Income Statement

Income Statement	2002–03	% of sales	2003–04	% of sales	2004–05	% of sales
Sales	$85,000*	100%	$140,000	100%	$160,000	
Cost of goods sold (COGS)						
• Merchandise	$45,050	53%	$74,200	53%	$84,800	53%
• Freight	$1,700	2%	$2,800	2%	$3,200	2%
Total COGS	**$46,750**	**55%**	**$77,000**	**55%**	**$88,000**	**55%**
Gross margin (sales - COGS)	$38,250	45%	$63,000	45%	$72,000	45%
Other income (such as grants)	$0		$0		$0	
Expenses						
• Operating expenses	$3,000	4%	$4,000	3%	$4,500	3%
• Salaries & fringe	$43,920	52%	$47,504	34%	$50,560	32%
• Interest expense	$3,600	4%	$2,880	2%	$2,160	1%
• Depreciation	$2,200	3%	$2,200	2%	$2,200	1%
Total expenses	**$52,720**	**62%**	**$56,584**	**40%**	**$59,420**	**37%**
Profit (gross margin - total expenses)	**($14,470)**	**17%**	**$6,416**	**5%**	**$12,580**	**8%**

* *Partial year (9 months). Store opens October 1, 2002.*

Three-Year Cash Flow Analysis

Summary Cash Flow Analysis	2002–03	2003–04	2004–05
Beginning cash balance	$0	$3,137	$503
✚ Add loan proceeds	$45,000		
▬ Deduct captial expense (build-out)	($11,000)		
✚ Add sales revenue	$85,000	$140,000	$160,000
▬ Deduct inventory purchases and freight	($65, 343)**	($77,000)	($88,000)
▬ Deduct expenses	($52,720)	($56,584)	($59,420)
✚ Add depreciation	$2,200	$2,200	$2,200
▬ Deduct principal payments	$0	($11,250)	($11,250)
Ending cash balance	**$3,137**	**$503**	**$4,033**

** *Includes approximately $19,000 for purchase of initial inventory*

Monthly Detailed Cash Flow Statements, 2002-03

	Jul	Aug	Sep	Oct	Nov	Dec	Jan	Feb	Mar	Apr	May	Jun	TOTALS
Beginning cash balance	0	38,700	22,609	6,226	2,343	1,906	3,039	1,532	1,090	1,090	7,066	7,924	
Bank loan	45,000												45,000
Internal loan					2,000		3,000	2,000				(7,000)	0
Space build out	(3,000)	(4,000)	(4,000)										
Sales revenue				8,500	7,500	9,500	5,000	4,500	7,500	15,000	13,500	14,000	85,000
Inventory purchase		(8,000)	(8,000)	(8,000)	(4,675)	(4,125)	(5,225)	(2,750)	(2,475)	(4,125)	(8,250)	(7,425)	(63,050)
Freight		(291)	(291)	(291)	(170)	(150)	(190)	(100)	(90)	(150)	(300)	(270)	(2,293)
Office supplies		(500)							(500)				(1,000)
Promotion					(1,000)					(1,000)			(2,000)
Salary and fringe	(3,000)	(3,000)	(3,792)	(3,792)	(3,792)	(3,792)	(3,792)	(3,792)	(3,792)	(3,792)	(3,792)	(3,792)	(43,920)
Loan payments	(300)	(300)	(300)	(300)	(300)	(300)	(300)	(300)	(300)	(300)	(300)	(300)	(3,600)
Ending cash balance	38,700	22,609	6,226	2,343	1,906	3,039	1,532	1,090	1,433	7,066	7,924	3,137	3,137

Sources-and-Uses-of-Financing Statement

The venture will secure a bank loan of $45,000, secured with Nature Center reserves, to pay for the following start-up costs: $11,000 to build out the space; $19,000 to purchase initial inventory; and $15,000 to address working capital (cash flow) requirements and other contingencies. The business plan assumes a five-year, 8% self-amortizing bank loan, with principal payments beginning in year two.

As indicated on the monthly cash flow statement, additional working capital requirements will be met through internal cash flow loans from the nature center. Those no-interest loans are estimated to equal $7,000 during the first year, to be repaid from operations by the end of that year.

Financial Summary

The gift shop is projected to generate sales of $85,000 during its first year, 2002-03 (partial year), increasing to $160,000 by year three. The gift shop is expected to lose $14,470 in the first year, and recover $6,416 of that in year two. In the third year it is projected to earn a profit of $12,580.

It is projected that during year one the gift shop will need additional working capital to cover monthly cash flow requirements. For that reason, the gift shop is expected to draw upon a no-interest, internal working capital line of credit of $7,000.

Breakeven Analysis

Using the percentage-of-sales method [Appendix F], and applying it to projected expenses for 2003-04 (the gift shop's first full year), breakeven is projected to occur as follows:

$$\text{Breakeven} = \text{Total annualized fixed costs} / \text{gross margin percentage}$$

$$\$56,584 / 45\% = \$125,742$$

In other words, breakeven is projected to occur on an annual basis once sales reach $125,742. Profits are earned if sales exceed that number, and losses occur if sales are below that level.

Note that the breakeven calculation will change if our fixed costs or gross margins change. For example, if fixed costs were to increase (say they went up $10,000), break-even would increase to $147,964 ($66,584/45%). Likewise, if the gross margin were to slip (say from 45% to 40%), breakeven would increase to $141,460 ($56,584/40%). Either change would turn a profitable year into a loss.

Notes to Financial Statements

General assumptions for income statements:

- Sales projections from industry data for nature or science center gift shops comparable in product mix and size. Third year (2004-05) projection based on multiplying sales of $1.50 per visitor (industry average for nature centers of our size) by the 120,000 visitors we receive each year. A second source is industry figure of $250 in net sales per square foot multiplied by the 700-square-foot gift shop that we're creating. To be conservative, we reduced the results of these calculations ($180,000 and $175,000 respectively) to $160,000.

- Merchandise and freight estimates are from ratios at stores with comparable product mixes. Merchandise cost estimated at 53% of sales (100% markup less discounts and shrinkage), and freight at 2% of sales.

- Operating expenses include supplies, postage, and promotion.

- Interest expense: $45,000 @ 8% interest = $3,600 (five-year bank loan to build out space ($11,000), buy initial inventory ($19,000), and cover working capital ($15,000)).

- Annual loan payments: $3,600 interest (first year, declines thereafter as balance is paid off) + $11,250 principal payment starting in 2003-04.

- Build-out expense ($11,000) is depreciated on a straight-line basis across five years.

- Internal allocation policies: consistent with other departments at the nature center, the gift shop will not be charged for rent, utilities, or phone service. Little or no additional expenses in these categories will be incurred as a result of opening the gift shop.

2002–03 (partial year) assumptions:

- Sales average $2,125/week for 40 weeks—Oct. 1, 2002 – June 30, 2003

- Salaries reflect four-fifths time store manager starting 7/1/02 at $36,000 including fringe, and assistant manager starting 9/1/02 at $7,920

2003–04 (first full year) assumptions:

- Weekly sales increase by 27%, expenses by 7%

- Average net sales of $2,692/week

- $2,000 (5.5%) increase in manager's compensation, including fringe and incentives. No change in assistant manager's compensation.

2004–05 assumptions:

- Sales increase by 14%, operating expenses by 6%

- Average net sales: $3,077/weekly

- $2,000 (5%) increase of manager's compensation, including fringe and incentives. Assistant manager's compensation (combination of additional hours and wage increase) grows to $10,560.

Appendix E
Unrelated Business Income Tax[*]

Even though an organization is recognized as tax exempt, it still may be liable for tax on its unrelated business income. Unrelated business income is income from a trade or business, regularly carried on, that is not substantially related to the performance by the organization of its exempt purpose or function except that the organization needs the profits derived from this activity. An exempt organization that has $1,000 or more gross income from an unrelated business must file Form 990-T, *Exempt Organization Business Income Tax Return.*

The unrelated business income tax (UBIT) applies to all organizations exempt from tax under Internal Revenue Code (IRC) section 501(a) except certain U.S. instrumentalities. State and municipal colleges and universities are also subject to UBIT.

All organizations subject to UBIT, except trusts, are taxable at corporate rates on that income. All exempt trusts that are subject to these provisions, and that, if not exempt, would be taxable as trusts, are taxable at trust rates on unrelated business taxable income. However, an exempt trust may not claim the deduction for a personal exemption that is normally allowed to a trust.

An activity will be considered an unrelated business (and subject to UBIT) if it meets the following three requirements: (1) it is a trade or business, (2) it is regularly carried on, and (3) it is not substantially related to the furtherance of the exempt purpose of the organization. However, there are a number of exclusions and modifications to this general rule.

[*] The material in Appendix E was downloaded from the Internal Revenue Service's web site, www.irs.gov/prod/bus_info/eo/unrel.html, on 3/8/01. Before making decisions on tax and legal issues, be sure to obtain current IRS information and consult with legal counsel.

The term "trade or business" generally includes any activity carried on for the production of income from selling goods or performing services. It is not limited to integrated aggregates of assets, activities, and goodwill that comprise businesses for the purposes of certain other provisions of the Internal Revenue Code. Activities of producing or distributing goods or performing services from which gross income is derived do not lose their identity as trades or businesses merely because they are carried on within a larger framework of other activities that may, or may not, be related to the exempt purposes of the organization.

Business activities of an exempt organization ordinarily will be considered to be "regularly carried on" if they show a frequency and continuity, and are pursued in a manner similar to comparable commercial activities of nonexempt organizations.

To determine whether a business activity is or is not "substantially related" requires an examination of the relationship between the business activities that generate the particular income in question and the accomplishment of the organization's exempt purpose. Trade or business is related to exempt purposes, in the statutory sense, only when the conduct of the business activities has causal relationship to the achievement of exempt purposes (other than through the production of income). The causal relationship must be substantial. The activities that generate the income must contribute importantly to the accomplishment of the organization's exempt purposes to be substantially related.

The Code contains a number of modifications, exclusions, and exceptions to unrelated business income. For example, dividends, interest, certain other investment income, royalties, certain rental income, certain income from research activities, and gains or losses from the disposition of property are excluded when computing unrelated business income. In addition, the following activities are also specifically excluded from the definition of unrelated trade or business:

- **Volunteer Labor**—Any trade or business is excluded in which substantially all the work is performed for the organization without compensation. Some fundraising activities, such as volunteer-operated bake sales, may meet this exception.

- **Convenience of Members**—Any trade or business is excluded that is carried on by an organization described in IRC section 501(c)(3) or by a governmental college or university primarily for the convenience of its members, students, patients, officers, or employees. A typical example of this would be a school cafeteria.

- **Selling Donated Merchandise**—Any trade or business is excluded that consists of selling merchandise, substantially all of which the organization received as gifts or contributions. Many thrift shop operations run by exempt organizations would meet this exception.

For a discussion of current developments concerning UBIT, download "UBIT: Current Developments." For a discussion of the special UBIT rules for organizations described in sections 501(c)(7), 501(c)(9), or 501(c)(17), see "Unrelated Business Income Tax." For more information, download "Publication 598," *Tax on Unrelated Business Income of Exempt Organizations,* available at www.irs.org.

Appendix F

Calculating Breakeven Using Percentage of Sales

There may be situations where the procedure for calculating breakeven (Worksheet 6B) does not line up with the venture you are evaluating. Examples include if you sell services at a wide and unpredictable variety of prices, or if some of your costs vary as a percentage of sales. This can occur if a salesperson is paid a commission as a percentage of the sales price. In that case, you will need to use a different approach to calculate breakeven, known as the "percentage-of-sales" method. In this approach, you express each of your variable costs as a percentage of the total sale. To make this clear, return to the focus group example used in sample Worksheets 6A and 6B (pages 105 and 109).

Sales	**always 100%**
Variable costs expressed as a percent of sales	
Cost to hire facilitator	15%
Space costs for focus groups	10%
Sales commission	5%
Food, parking, etc.	5%
Total variable costs as a percentage of sales	**35%**
Gross margin percentage	
(Sales percent minus total variable costs percent)	**65%**

If you assume the same fixed costs as in sample Worksheet 6A (page 105):

Breakeven = Total annualized fixed costs / gross margin percentage
        = $32,500 / 65%
        = $50,000

In this case, breakeven is determined relative to sales rather than units sold. The business needs to sell $50,000 worth of focus groups each year in order to achieve breakeven. Profitability occurs when sales exceed $50,000.

Appendix G
Blank Worksheets

Electronic versions of these worksheets may be downloaded from the publisher's web site. Use the following URL and code to obtain the worksheets

http://www.fieldstonealliance.org/worksheets

Code: W245VF02

These online worksheets are intended for use in the same way as photocopies of the worksheets, but they are in a form that allows you to type in your responses and reformat the worksheets to fit your final business plan. Please do not download the worksheets unless you or your organization has purchased this workbook. If you have any trouble downloading the files, please call the publisher at 800-274-6024.

Instructions

❑ Prepare a draft of Worksheet 1A and Worksheet 1B.

❑ Discuss them with your venture team and the executive director.

❑ Revise as needed.

Mission

1. What is your nonprofit's mission? How does the organization carry out that mission?

2. Apart from generating income, how do you anticipate that ventures might help you pursue your nonprofit mission?

Money

3. What amount and percentage of your annual budget currently comes from earned income activities? What are the sources for this income? What is the profit or loss from that income, and how is that measured?

Total budget

Earned amount

Earned percent

(continued)

4. In five years, if growth in ventures proves successful, how would you expect these figures to change? A common preliminary target is to increase earned income by ten percentage points.

Estimated total budget in five years

Earned income amount

Earned income percent

Capacity

5. Describe how ventures might enhance your organizational skills and capabilities.

- Raise the organization's visibility and reputation

- Enhance our ability to understand our customers

- Expand our ability to analyze program costs and effectiveness

- Provide opportunities for staff to build new skills

- Other:

Concerns

6. What concerns do you have about pursuing ventures? What can you do to address those concerns?

Instructions

❑ Prepare a draft process and timeline.

❑ Discuss with venture team and executive director.

❑ Revise as needed.

Step	Start date	Completion date
1. Get organized *Present plan to board*		
2. Conduct a venture audit		
3. Brainstorm and screen venture ideas *Entrepreneurial committee meeting #1*		
4. Perform quick market tests *Entrepreneurial committee meeting #2*		
5. Do feasibility market research *Entrepreneurial committee meeting #3*		
6. Prepare feasibility financial analysis *Entrepreneurial committee meeting #4* *Present feasibility study to board*		
7. Write a business plan *Entrepreneurial committee meeting #5* *Present business plan to board*		

Instructions

❑ Complete the following table identifying the members of the venture team, their duties, and the estimated amount of their time that will be needed to work on this project.

❑ Ask each team member to review and initial to confirm their role in the project.

❑ Similarly, request that your executive director approve and sign off on the project objectives of Worksheet 1A and process and timeline of Worksheet 1B.

Venture Project Team Roster:

Title	Name	Project duties	Estimated time	Agreed (initials)
Project leader				
Team member				
Team member				
Team member				
Team member				
Team member				
Team member				
Team member				

Venture Project Approvals:

Name	Position	Approved (initials)

Instructions

❑ Consider as constituents any community of people or organizations that you now serve.

❑ While it is appropriate to list specific names, try to describe each constituency in terms that could encompass others who are related in some fashion. For example, you could name "Oakdale School District," and expand that to "west metro school districts."

❑ Ignore internal constituents such as staff and board since they are unlikely to become customers for your ventures.

1. Who are your constituents? How do they interact with your organization?
   For now, don't worry about overlap between categories.

Constituency	Interaction with your nonprofit and how you provide *value* to *them*

2. What in general do you know about these constituents?
   Divide into segments as needed to clarify differences.

Constituency	Overall characteristics (by segment if appropriate)

(continued)

3. Which of these constituencies or segments represent core customers for your organization? Consider whether you know enough about them to envision products or services that they might want, and whether they are likely to have the ability to pay for such products. Rate on a scale of 1 to 5, where 5 is Yes, 4 is Probably, 3 is Uncertain, 2 is Probably Not, and 1 is No. Why?

Constituency	Core customers?

4. Finally, are there any other prospective customers who are not current constituents of your nonprofit, but with whom your organization has a natural link and who therefore should be included as you consider new venture possibilities?

Prospective customer	Why? How are we linked to them?

Instructions

❑ Describe how your nonprofit makes a special difference to the community, using words that would make sense to those you serve. Aim for six to twelve possible competencies.

❑ For each competency, list: (1) why your core customers value this; (2) a variety of customers who value or are likely to value this; and (3) why it is difficult for others to imitate.

❑ After the meeting, sift through the list, eliminating or sharpening points that are too general ("quality staff," "good service," "relationship-based"), use insider jargon, or don't meet the three-part core competency test. Then refine and reduce the list to a manageable number (three or four is best, no more than six) that can be reviewed and approved.

Competency:

Why your customers value this	Variety of customers who value (or are likely to value) this	Why it is difficult for others to imitate

Instructions

❑ Rank each question according to the following scale. (A scoring key appears at the end.)

5 = yes	4 = probably	3 = maybe	2 = probably not	1 = no

Rating

1. Do you have the financial stability and budget flexibility to invest sufficient resources (at least one-third full-time employee for six months) into exploring venture opportunities?

   Explain:

   _____

2. If a promising venture opportunity emerges and a business plan is written, can you invest staff and financial resources into launching that venture?

   Explain:

   _____

3. Do you have strong financial and accounting capability on staff?

   Explain:

   _____

4. Do you have strong financial and accounting capability on the board?

   Explain:

   _____

5. Do you have strong marketing background and experience on staff?

   Explain:

   _____

6. Do you have strong marketing background and experience on the board?

   Explain:

   _____

Rating

7. Do you have staff stability and continuity (slow turnover), especially for the three most senior positions in the organization? _____

   Explain:

8. Does your organizational culture encourage innovation, risk taking, and long-term thinking? _____

   Explain:

9. Do the executive director and the board support the development of earned income ventures? _____

   Explain:

10. Do you have a solid internal cost-accounting system that provides reliable data on fixed and variable costs for each program or activity? _____

    Explain:

11. Do you have the ability to establish the cost for a unit of service? _____

    Explain:

Total score _____

SCORING <33 Weak 34–38 Fair 39–43 Good 44+ Excellent

Instructions

❑ With help from the venture team, mentally browse through your organization, looking for tangible and intangible assets that are valued or might be valued by paying customers.

❑ Discuss each asset, and decide which ones show enough potential to be placed on the worksheet.

Asset	Potential customers	Why they might be interested and willing to pay

Instructions

❑ The executive director is probably the best person to address constituency concerns.
Discuss this worksheet with him or her, and then fill out a summary.

Funders

1. Who are your most important funders?

2. How do you anticipate that each would respond if your organization decides
to set up a venture? Would it matter what kind of a venture?

Board

3. How will your board react?

Allies

4. How about key nonprofit allies—are there any that would challenge your decision
to launch a venture? Would that represent a threat to your organization?

Rivals

5. Are there nonprofit or for-profit rivals that could also challenge such a decision?
Would that represent a threat?

Instructions

❑ At the entrepreneurial committee meeting, review the venture audit, Venture Brainstorming Pyramid, (page 46) and brainstorming guidelines (page 45).

❑ Emphasize that while the goal is to look for venture ideas that would build on your audit strengths, all ideas are welcome.

❑ Ask that ideas indicate customer group, product or service idea, and likely customer benefits. (See chart below.)

❑ Write down each of the brainstormed ideas including target customers. Refer to the pyramid to make sure most of the ideas come from the bottom half.

❑ After the meeting, the project leader should write up the list, rewording vague ideas and eliminating clearly impractical ideas.

Customer group	Product or service ideas	Customer benefits

Instructions

❏ Create a summary table similar to the one below, along with additional notes on an attached page if necessary to explain the concept.

❏ Present the list to your venture team, and then mail it to the entrepreneurial committee to solicit their votes.

❏ Tally up the votes during the entrepreneurial committee meeting, and lead a discussion on what the numbers suggest, and where they may be off the mark.

❏ At that meeting, or subsequently with the venture team, select no more than three venture ideas to undergo the quick market test.

❏ Rank each venture according to the following scale.

5 = yes	4 = probably	3 = maybe	2 = probably not	1 = no

Venture idea	Criteria						Total

Instructions

❏ Use a separate worksheet for each venture idea.

❏ Answer as many questions as you can with available information; then design a QMT research plan (Worksheet 4B) to fill in gaps and verify your information.

❏ Based on your research findings, complete this worksheet.

Name of Venture:

Product

1. Clearly describe the proposed product or service.

2. How will you produce and deliver it?

3. How will customers find it beneficial to them?

Customers

4. Who are your target customers?

5. What relationship do you have with your target customers?

6. What evidence do you have of customer interest?

7. How will you sell this product to these customers?

8. Are they growing in numbers or buying more each year?

9. What is important to these customers?

Advantages

10. How does this venture build on your core competencies?

11. How will you produce and deliver this product efficiently?

12. What is the competition for this product?

13. How difficult would it be for another firm to replicate your product?

(continued)

14. Why would customers prefer your product?

15. How does this idea fit with your mission and the attitude of key stakeholders?

Business Model

16. What evidence do you have that customers will pay for this and that there is profit potential?

17. What are the start-up costs for this venture and where will the funding come from?

18. What is the minimum sales level needed to make a profit?

19. What weaknesses will your nonprofit face in running this venture?

20. What staff (both managerial and operational) will you need to operate this venture?

Instructions

❑ Use a separate worksheet for each venture idea.

❑ From Worksheet 4A, draft answers to the questions and then identify gaps and areas requiring more research.

❑ With help from the venture team, other staff, and informal advice from the entrepreneurial committee, use Worksheet 4B to identify how those gaps will get filled.

❑ Do the research, and use the results to complete Worksheets 4A and 4C.

1. What is the venture idea, what is the product or service, and who are the target customers?

2. Who will be interviewed and who will conduct each interview?

3. What published sources will be used and who will be responsible for finding them?

4. What Internet sources will be used and who will be responsible for finding them?

5. How many hours will be put into this, and by what date will the research be completed?

Instructions

❑ Use the information from your completed QMT Twenty Questions worksheet (4A) to rate each of your answers.

❑ Use the following ratings to make your evaluation. (A scoring key appears at the end.)

5 = yes	4 = probably	3 = maybe	2 = probably not	1 = no

Product   **Rating**

1. Can you clearly describe the product or service?   _____

2. Do you know how to produce and deliver it?   _____

3. Do you know how customers will find it beneficial to them?   _____

Customers

4. Have you identified your target customers?   _____

5. Do you have an existing relationship with these customers?   _____

6. Do you have evidence of customer interest?   _____

7. Do you know how to sell this product to these customers?   _____

8. Are they growing in numbers or buying more each year?   _____

9. Do you know what's important to these customers?   _____

Advantages

10. Does this venture build on your core competencies?   _____

11. Could you produce and deliver it efficiently?   _____

12. Do you know what the competition is for this product?   _____

13. Would it be difficult for another firm to replicate your product? _____

14. Is there good reason to expect customers would prefer your product? _____

15. Does this represent a good fit with your mission and key stakeholders? _____

Business Model	**Rating**
16. Do you have evidence that customers will pay for this and that there is profit potential?	_____
17. Could you tolerate, finance, or raise the start-up costs for this venture?	_____
18. Do you know the minimum sales level needed to make a profit?	_____
19. Can you overcome weaknesses your nonprofit will have running this venture?	_____
20. Can you find suitable staff (managerial and operational) to operate this venture?	_____
Total score	_____

SCORING

74+ Impressive! Looks like you're on to something. Proceed to the feasibility study, or, if start-up costs and risks are low, prepare a brief plan, a budget, and *just do it*.

69–73 Gray area. Review the customer and advantage sections carefully before deciding to do a full feasibility study on this idea.

59–68 Probably drop it. Exceptions would be if there are several "0" ratings that, with additional research or revising the concept, might change to higher scores.

< 58 Drop it.

Instructions

❏ Go through the worksheets for Step 5 and fill in what you can.

❏ Note gaps in the worksheets and where verification is needed.

❏ Using this worksheet, develop a research plan to fill in those gaps.

1. How will you directly contact target customers to evaluate their interest in and willingness to pay for your products or services? (Examples include informal contact, interviews, surveys, and focus groups.)

2. What knowledgeable people can you contact to get more information about these target customers?

3. What trade associations, government agencies, or chambers of commerce will you contact for information about this industry?

4. What industry experts, consultants, or suppliers will you contact for information about this industry?

5. Who else in the industry (preferably noncompetitors) will you contact for information about this industry?

6. What kinds of "secret shopping" will you do of competitors to get a feel for their offerings and marketing strategies?

7. What kinds of library and Internet research will you undertake to improve your understanding of this industry?

8. What other sources of information will you draw on to help answer the questions in Step 5?

Instructions

❑ Fill in what you already know about your target customers. Identify where the gaps are and where additional verification is needed.

❑ Note the gaps as you develop and carry out your feasibility research plan (Worksheet 5A).

❑ Return to this worksheet and fill in the gaps.

1. Who are the target customers for this venture? Be specific. *Profile* them. What's the *size* of each segment? What's the growth *trend* in this segment: fast growing, slow growing, stable, or declining? (Fast-growing segments increase by at least 10 percent per year.) What *benefits* do these customers perceive from this venture?

Customer segment	Description
	Profile: Size: Trend: Benefits:
	Profile: Size: Trend: Benefits:
	Profile: Size: Trend: Benefits:

2. What products would interest these customers?

3. How do customers typically get information about these types of products?
   Are there intermediaries through whom this kind of a venture tends to attract customers?

Instructions

❏ Fill in what you already know and what you still need to find out.
   Identify where your information gaps are.

❏ Use the information you gather while doing market research (Worksheet 5A)
   to complete your answers to these questions.

1. Detail the evidence demonstrating that your target customers will be interested in purchasing these products. Who else is selling related products that suggests this could be successful?

2. What trends in the marketplace provide further evidence that you will be able to sell these products to these customers?

3. Finally, what does your research into customer interest tell you about the likely quantity of annual customers and sales for each of the customer segments? Consider what this might be after the venture is "fully established," which is typically after two or three years of operation.

Instructions

❑ Fill in what you already know and what you still need to find out. Identify the gaps in the information.

❑ Don't worry if you're not sure in which category a given success factor belongs; pick the one it fits in best.

❑ Use the information you gathered while doing market research (Worksheet 5A) to complete your answers to these questions.

1. What are the *customer* success factors for this venture idea?

Customer success factor	Why does this matter to customers?

(continued)

2. What are the *marketing* success factors for this venture idea?

Marketing success factor	Why is this essential for success with this venture?

3. What are the *operational* success factors for this venture idea?

Operational success factor	Why is this essential for success with this venture?

Instructions

❏ Fill in what you already know. Identify what you still need to find out for this worksheet.

❏ Use the information you gathered while carrying out your feasibility market research plan (Worksheet 5A) to complete your answers to these questions.

❏ Questions about competitor pricing strategies appear in Worksheet 5I.

1. Who are the most likely competitors for your business and its target customers? Consider all types of competition as described on page 81 under the heading "Profile primary competitors." Indicate how the competition may be different for each of your customer segments.

Customer segment	Similar product and experience	Similar product, different experience	Same customers, different offerings	Other alternatives
Segment 1				
Segment 2				
Segment 3				
Segment 4				

(continued)

2. Which of these do you consider to be your primary competitors? Why? (Pick at least three competitors who present the closest similarity with your venture, first in terms of customers—the alternative they would most likely choose if your venture ceased to exist—and second in terms of products or services. Explain why each one was picked.)

3. Construct a brief profile of *each* of your primary competitors, including customers, size, products or services, and areas of strength or special appeal.

4. Describe the communication strategies that each primary competitor uses for its marketing efforts.

Instructions

❏ Pull out your answers to Worksheets 5D (Success Factors) and 5E (Competitor Profiles). Place them on a grid with your business and the competition across the top and success factors along the side.

❏ Using this information, and what you know about your organization and its capabilities, complete the remainder of the worksheet.

1. From Worksheet 5D, what are the success factors for this venture idea?

2. From Worksheet 5E, who will your key competitors be?

(continued)

3. On each of the success factors, how will you compare with these competitors? It is important to be objective and realistic rather than promotional. With rare exceptions, only one organization can be ranked with a "5" as market leader for any success factor. If you find that your answers will differ markedly by customer segment, create a separate table for each segment.

Segment:

Competitor: 5 = major strength   4 = strength   3 = neutral   2 = weakness   1 = major weakness

Success factor:	Us			
Total score				

4. What does this table (and other data you have gathered) indicate about the relative strengths of your key competitors?

5. What are *your* competitive advantages?

6. What are your competitive disadvantages?

(continued)

Instructions

❑ Using Target Customers (Worksheet 5B), Customer Interest (5C), Success Factors (5D), and Competitor Profiles (5E), and with help from other members of your venture team, answer the following questions.

❑ If you have difficulty answering the questions, you may need to do more market research.

1. What did you identify in Worksheet 5D as the key customer and marketing success factors for this venture idea?

2. What did you identify about customer interests in Worksheets 5B and 5C that might suggest marketing requirements for this venture idea? Separate by customer segments if appropriate.

3. What communication strategies of competitors did you identify in question 4 of Worksheet 5E?

4. As identified in your research, what communication strategies are used by similar but noncompeting firms—for example, businesses in another city, or businesses that target the same customer segments but with different products?

5. Now, review your list of competitors (Worksheet 5E, question 1). There were probably several that you did *not* describe as primary competitors (Worksheet 5E, question 2). Considering those secondary competitors (whom your customers will sometimes perceive as their alternatives), are there marketing requirements to increase the odds that they will come to you rather than pursue these alternatives?

(continued)

6. What advice about marketing requirements have you obtained from industry experts, trade associations, or consultants working in this area?

7. Finally, how would you translate the above information into a set of marketing requirements for this venture idea? Include requirements for ongoing marketing *research* (e.g., customer surveys, competitor analysis) as well as for communication *strategies* (such as promotional efforts).

Instructions

❑ With help from other members of your venture team, answer the following questions. Use Worksheet 5D: Success Factors and Worksheet 5E: Competitor Profiles for details.

❑ It's not uncommon to have difficulty answering some of the questions. This indicates a need for more market research. If your research is adequate, the worksheet should go quickly.

1. What did you identify in Worksheet 5D as the key operational success factors for this venture idea? Also list any customer and marketing success factors that have an operational component to them (they usually do).

2. **Facility:** What type of facility will be needed to satisfy the success factors? If you expect to use space the nonprofit currently has control over, what improvements will be needed? If new space will be needed, what are the requirements for that space?

3. **Equipment:** What kinds of equipment will be needed to run this venture and to meet the success factors?

(continued)

4. **Production Processes:** What types of production processes or activities will be needed to create products and prepare them for sale in a way that satisfies the success factors?

5. **Supply Chain:** What relationships with suppliers and other providers will be required to run the venture and satisfy the success factors?

6. **Staffing:** What type and level of staffing will be needed to operate this venture in a manner that meets the success factors?

7. **Key Ratios:** What are the key operational and financial ratios that experienced managers in this industry track and manage to ensure success? What kinds of results does your research indicate you need to achieve with this venture?

Instructions

❑ With help from other members of your venture team, answer the following questions. Use Worksheet 5C: Customer Interest and Worksheet 5E: Competitor Profiles for necessary details.

❑ If you have difficulty answering the questions, you may need to do more market research.

1. Are there industry standards or practices that firms in this business tend to follow?

2. How do your primary competitors price their products? What can you ascertain about their pricing strategies?

(continued)

3. What do your target customers appear willing to pay for your proposed products? You should be able to obtain this information from your answers to Worksheet 5C.

4. What will it cost your organization to produce a product or service unit? (If this information is not readily available or requires some calculations, skip this question for now; details on how to calculate this can be found in the financials section of Step 6.)

5. Based on all of the above information, what would you state as the key pricing requirements for this venture idea?

Instructions

❑ Review the earlier worksheets in this step to see if any requirements have been missed.

❑ Using this information, and with help from other members of your venture team, answer the following questions.

❑ If you have difficulty answering the questions, you may need to do more market research.

1. What other requirements are needed to operate this venture?

2. Has legal counsel informed you about any legal requirements that you need to be mindful of?

Instructions

❏ Based on your research and the requirements worksheets in Step 5, create a one-year budget to start up and operate this venture.

❏ Next, separate out variable costs from fixed costs. For fixed costs, identify how long it will be before the cost will be incurred again.

1. What are the annual fixed costs to start up and operate this venture for one year?

To make this calculation, first list each fixed cost along with its "useful life." For those costs that cover more than one year, enter only the first year's costs. To compute the first year's costs, divide the total cost by the number of years (its useful life). For example, if you pay $1,500 for a copy machine with a three-year life, you would assign $500 as the annual fixed cost. Expenses of this sort are often referred to as capital expenses.

Fixed costs	Annual amount	Useful life in years
Total annual fixed costs		

2. What will the variable costs be for the products this venture will sell? You may need to make an assumption about average price per unit.

Estimated variable cost	Cost
Total variable costs per unit	

3. Optional: Summarize fixed and variable costs graphically. Dollars form the vertical axis and sales units form the horizontal axis. Graph the fixed costs first; they will form a horizontal line. Graph the total costs next; they will form an ascending line rising above the fixed costs. The space between the fixed costs and the total costs is a graphic representation of variable costs.

Total Costs

Fixed Costs

Instructions

❑ Pull out Worksheet 6A: Budget.

❑ Answer the questions to come up with an estimated breakeven for this venture idea.

❑ Do a "reality check" on the result (i.e., does this seem possible?) and on the supporting data (i.e., have you been realistic about costs?).

1. What is the average unit price for your product? (From Worksheet 6A, question 2.)

2. What is the variable cost per unit? (From Worksheet 6A, question 2.)

3. What is the gross margin per unit?
   Gross margin per unit = average unit price - variable cost per unit

4. What are the estimated annual fixed costs for this product? (Worksheet 6A, question 1.)

5. Using the formula indicated below, when do you achieve breakeven? What does this tell you?
   Breakeven = total fixed costs / gross margin per unit

6. Check your results by calculating profit if sales equal breakeven. If sales equal the breakeven quantity, profits should be zero (or close to zero depending on rounding errors).

	Units	Cost
Total sales		
Less total variable costs		
Gross margin		
Less total fixed costs		
Profit (loss)		

7. Estimate profit and loss if you sell quantities greater or less than breakeven. What does this tell you?

	Units If we sell _____	Cost	Units If we sell _____	Cost
Total sales at $_____ per unit				
Less variable costs at $_____ per unit				
Gross margin				
Less total fixed costs				
Profit (loss)				

(continued)

8. Optional: Present profits and losses graphically. Dollars form the vertical axis and units sold form the horizontal axis. Graph the fixed costs, the total costs, and the sales. (Use the graphic created in Worksheet 6A as a starting point.) The point at which the sales line crosses over the variable costs line represents the beginning of profitability.

9. Reality check: Do these results seem plausible? It's all right if you don't know, but if the numbers seem outside the range of possibility, now is the time to evaluate whether to proceed to the next worksheet. Similarly, are you confident that you have been realistic about costs? One way to measure this: Do you have about as much confidence in this budget as you have in your nonprofit's annual budget (or your department, if that's a better comparison)?

Instructions

❑ **Revenues**: Based on your previous research, what's a conservative estimate of sales for each of the first three years of operations?

❑ **Costs**: Taking the costs you identified in Worksheets 6A and 6B, what do you estimate those costs will be for each of the first three years?

❑ **Projections**: With help from a finance person (if needed), prepare an initial draft of your financial projections using a computer spreadsheet program. Be sure to prepare a cash flow statement as well as an income statement. Discuss them with your venture team, and then make adjustments as appropriate.

❑ **Financing**: Based on your projections, how much financing will be required to launch and operate this venture for its first three years?

❑ **Notes**: Prepare notes to your financial statements, listing your assumptions and how you calculated your projections.

Income Statement	Year: _____	% of sales	Year: _____	% of sales	Year: _____	% of sales
Sales						
Cost of goods sold (COGS)						
• Merchandise						
• Freight						
Total COGS						
Gross margin (sales – COGS)						
Other income (such as grants)						
Expenses						
• Operating expenses						
• Salaries & fringe						
• Interest expense						
• Depreciation						
Total expenses						
Profit (gross margin - total expenses)						

(continued)

Summary Cash Flow Analysis	Year:	Year:	Year:
Beginning cash balance			
+ Add loan proceeds			
− Deduct captial expense (build-out)			
+ Add sales revenue			
− Deduct inventory purchases and freight			
− Deduct expenses			
+ Add depreciation			
− Deduct principal payments			
Ending cash balance			

Financial Summary

Instructions

❏ Meet with your venture team to discuss risks and uncertainties.

❏ List in this worksheet those that seem most significant.

1. What risk will you face if sales are lower than anticipated? What would happen if sales were down 10 percent or even 25 percent from your projections?

2. What is the risk that costs will be higher than expected? Consider both variable and fixed costs.

(continued)

3. What is the risk that prices you have assumed are too high, and that you'll need to reduce your prices to attract customers and remain competitive?

4. What are the risks if it proves difficult to attract suitable workers for this venture?

5. What other important risks and uncertainties can you anticipate? How serious are these risks?

6. Among the risks indicated above, which are the most serious?

7. If the venture's financial results were significantly worse than projected, what would be done? What steps would be taken to reduce costs? At what point would the venture be shut down? How difficult (financially and otherwise) would that be for the organization?

Instructions

❏ Pull out your Worksheet 6C: Financial Projections and Summary and Worksheet 6D: Risks.

❏ Prepare written summaries as requested in this worksheet.

1. What are your sales and profit projections for the first three years operating this venture idea? (Retrieve from Worksheet 6C.)

2. What are the most important underlying factors driving these numbers?

3. How confident are you that these results can be achieved? What's the margin of uncertainty?

4. What are the most significant risks and uncertainties facing this venture idea? Why do you believe these uncertainties either will not occur or can be overcome?

5. Based on all of your feasibility analysis (Steps 5 and 6), does the evidence support a conclusion that this venture appears sufficiently feasible to justify a decision to write a business plan to commence operations?

Instructions

❏ Identify the audience for the business plan. Whose approval will be needed before the venture can be launched?

❏ Write down what they will be looking for in the plan; if you're uncertain, ask them.

1. Who is the audience for this business plan?

2. What will they be looking for in the plan?

3. How will they evaluate the plan?

4. Who will be responsible for preparing the business plan?
   What are his or her qualifications to do this work?

Instructions

❏ Pull out your completed worksheets for Steps 5 and 6.

❏ Fill out what you can below; return to fill in the gaps once you've finished the remaining worksheets in Step 7.

1. Summarize the nonprofit's mission, services, and role in the community.

2. What prior experience and expertise does the nonprofit have—in terms of core competencies, resources, and management and marketing capabilities—to operate a successful venture? To help with this question, refer to the information gathered for Step 2, Conduct a Venture Audit.

(continued)

3. In a nutshell, what is this business all about? Who will the customers be, and what evidence is there that they will be willing to pay for something like this? Most of this information can be found in your feasibility research. (Summarize from Worksheets 5B and 5C.)

4. Who will manage, market, and operate this venture? Why will their backgrounds and experience ensure its success?

5. What revenues do you expect from this venture? When do you expect to reach breakeven and at what sales volume level? What will it cost (start-up expenses plus initial losses) to get to that point? How profitable will it become? (Retrieve from Worksheet 6C.)

6. What are the most significant risks that could undermine success with this venture, and what will be done to overcome them?

Instructions

❑ Pull out your completed worksheets for Steps 5 and 6.

❑ Cut and paste, editing as needed, to complete this worksheet.

1. What products will be sold via this venture? (Retrieve from Worksheet 5B, question 2.)

2. Who are the target customers for these products? Be specific. Compare and contrast the various customer groups that will be targeted. What benefits will these customers perceive from purchasing these products? (Retrieve from Worksheet 5B, question 1.)

Customer segment	Description
	Profile: Size: Trend: Benefits:
	Profile: Size: Trend: Benefits:

Customer segment	Description
	Profile:
	Size:
	Trend:
	Benefits:

3. Detail the *evidence* demonstrating that the target customers will be interested in purchasing these products. (Summarize from Worksheet 5C, question 1.)

4. Who else is successfully selling similar products to comparable target customers that suggests this could be successful? (Also from Worksheet 5C, question 1.)

(continued)

5. What trends in the marketplace provide further evidence that you will be able to sell these products to these customers? (Summarize from Worksheet 5C, question 2.)

6. How many customers and how much in annual sales will you obtain from these customers? (Retrieve from Worksheet 5C, question 3.)

7. What is it about your organization or your products that will make it likely that these customers will buy from you?

8. For your target customers, who are the most likely primary competitors? (Summarize from Worksheet 5E.)

9. How will you make money from this venture?

Instructions

❑ Answer the questions below to identify the people who will manage the venture and their responsibilities.

1. Who will be in charge of this venture activity? Why is he or she well-suited for this assignment? (Tie this to the needs of the venture—do not simply write "see attached resume and job description.")

2. Who else will be on the management team carrying out the responsibilities of this venture? What skills do they have—tied in again to the needs of the venture—that will enable this to be a successful business?

3. How will this activity be structured within the nonprofit? In other words, who will the person in charge of it report to? Where will the venture be situated in the organizational chart?

4. Who else inside and outside the organization will this venture work with to accomplish its goals?

Instructions

❏ Pull out your Worksheet 5H: Operational Requirements.

❏ For each category, work out the details on how this venture will meet each requirement.

1. **Facility.** Where specifically will this venture be located? Are there other locations where work takes place? What improvements does the facility need? How does this location and the facility meet the requirements as stated in the feasibility study? What are the costs associated with acquiring and preparing this facility?

2. **Equipment.** What specific equipment or technology will be needed? How will this meet the equipment requirements? What will it cost to purchase and install this equipment?

(continued)

3. **Production processes.** How will the venture physically produce and deliver these products? How will this meet the process requirements? What costs are associated with these processes?

4. **Supply Chain.** How and from whom will this venture obtain the supplies it needs to be successful? How does this meet the supply chain requirements? What costs are expected from this?

5. **Staffing.** How will you meet the staffing requirements for this business? What do you anticipate your staffing costs will be?

Instructions

❏ Review Worksheet 5G: Marketing Requirements.

❏ Make decisions on your marketing strategies.

1. What are the marketing goals for this venture?

2. What are the key marketing requirements to succeed in attracting target customers?
   (Lift this answer from question 7 of Worksheet 5G.)

3. How will this venture be positioned relative to your competitors? How will you price your products, and how will that compare to your competitors' pricing?

4. What communication strategies will be undertaken to satisfy the marketing requirements and your positioning statement? What is the timetable for these activities? What strategies will focus on getting repeat business from existing customers as opposed to attracting new customers?

5. What will it cost to carry out these activities? What's the timeline for these efforts?

6. Who will evaluate the effectiveness of these marketing efforts? How and when will they do so?

Instructions

❑ Decide on a target start date for the business.

❑ Write down what needs to be completed by that date. For help, refer back to Worksheet 7E: Operational Plan and 7F: Marketing Plan.

❑ For each item on your list, determine how much lead time is required, how it will be done, and who will be responsible for completing it. Keep in mind that some items need to be completed before work on other items can begin.

1. What is the target date for the business to commence operations? How fixed is that date— what are the consequences if the start is delayed?

2. What are the key tasks that need to be completed in order to launch the business on the target date? What is the timeline for each task? How will each part get done—and by whom? Refer to your operational (Worksheet 7E) and marketing (Worksheet 7F) plans.

Instructions

❑ Review Worksheet 6C: Financial Projections and Summary, which you prepared in Step 6.

❑ Update and make any corrections needed to reflect decisions made in the business plan.

❑ Prepare the following tables and insert in the order outlined below:

- Insert Three-Year Income Statement

- Insert Three-Year Cash Flow Analysis

- Insert Monthly Detailed Cash Flow Statements, Year 1

- Insert Sources-and-Uses-of-Financing Statement

- Insert Financial Summary

- Insert Breakeven Analysis

- Insert Notes to Financial Statements

Instructions

❏ Pull out Worksheet 6D: Risks.

❏ For each of the key risks identified in that worksheet, describe how you will minimize the chance of the event occurring, or how you would respond if it were to occur.

1. What are the most serious risks that were identified in Worksheet 6D? Are there any other serious risks that you have become aware of since doing that worksheet?

2. Why do you believe these risks are not so worrisome that the business should not be started?

3. What will you do to minimize the likelihood that these risks will be realized and create a problem for the business?

4. If these risks do occur, what steps will you take to prevent them from harming the business?

Index

More results-oriented books from Fieldstone Alliance

Finance

Bookkeeping Basics
What Every Nonprofit Bookkeeper Needs to Know
by Debra L. Ruegg and Lisa M. Venkatrathnam

Complete with step-by-step instructions, a glossary of accounting terms, detailed examples, and handy reproducible forms, this book will enable you to successfully meet the basic bookkeeping requirements of your nonprofit organization—even if you have little or no formal accounting training.

128 pages, softcover   Item # 069296

Coping with Cutbacks
The Nonprofit Guide to Success When Times Are Tight
by Emil Angelica and Vincent Hyman

Shows you practical ways to involve business, government, and other nonprofits to solve problems together. Also includes 185 cutback strategies you can put to use right away.

128 pages, softcover   Item # 069091

Financial Leadership for Nonprofit Executives
Guiding Your Organization to Long-term Success
by Jeanne Peters and Elizabeth Schaffer

Provides executives with a practical guide to protecting and growing the assets of their organizations and with accomplishing as much mission as possible with those resources.

144 pages, softcover   Item # 06944X

Venture Forth! The Essential Guide to Starting a Moneymaking Business in Your Nonprofit Organization
by Rolfe Larson

The most complete guide on nonprofit business development. Building on the experience of dozens of organizations, this handbook gives you a time-tested approach for finding, testing, and launching a successful nonprofit business venture.

272 pages, softcover   Item # 069245

Marketing

The Wilder Nonprofit Field Guide to
Conducting Successful Focus Groups
by Judith Sharken Simon

Shows how to collect valuable information without a lot of money or special expertise. Using this proven technique, you'll get essential opinions and feedback to help you check out your assumptions, do better strategic planning, improve services or products, and more.

80 pages, softcover   Item # 069199

Marketing Workbook for Nonprofit Organizations Volume I: Develop the Plan
by Gary J. Stern

Don't just wish for results—get them! Here's how to create a straightforward, usable marketing plan. Includes the six Ps of Marketing, how to use them effectively, a sample marketing plan, tips on using the Internet, and worksheets.

208 pages, softcover   Item # 069253

Marketing Workbook for Nonprofit Organizations Volume II: Mobilize People for Marketing Success
by Gary J. Stern

Put together a successful promotional campaign based on the most persuasive tool of all: personal contact. Learn how to mobilize your entire organization, its staff, volunteers, and supporters in a focused, one-to-one marketing campaign. Comes with *Pocket Guide for Marketing Representatives*. In it, your marketing representatives can record key campaign messages and find motivational reminders.

192 pages, softcover   Item # 069105

Management & Leadership

Benchmarking for Nonprofits
How to Measure, Manage, and Improve Results
by Jason Saul

This book defines a formal, systematic, and reliable way to benchmark (the onging process of measuring your organization against leaders), from preparing your organization to measuring performance and implementing best practices.

128 pages, softcover   Item # 069431

Consulting with Nonprofits: A Practitioner's Guide
by Carol A. Lukas

A step-by-step, comprehensive guide for consultants. Addresses the art of consulting, how to run your business, and much more. Also includes tips and anecdotes from thirty skilled consultants.

240 pages, softcover   Item # 069172

The Wilder Nonprofit Field Guide to
Crafting Effective Mission and Vision Statements
by Emil Angelica

Guides you through two six-step processes that result in a mission statement, vision statement, or both. Shows how a clarified mission and vision lead to more effective leadership, decisions, fundraising, and management. Includes tips, sample statements, and worksheets.

88 pages, softcover   Item # 06927X

For current prices, a catalog, or to order call ☎ 800-274-6024

The Wilder Nonprofit Field Guide to
Developing Effective Teams
by Beth Gilbertsen and Vijit Ramchandani

Helps you understand, start, and maintain a team. Provides tools and techniques for writing a mission statement, setting goals, conducting effective meetings, creating ground rules to manage team dynamics, making decisions in teams, creating project plans, and developing team spirit.

80 pages, softcover   Item # 069202

The Five Life Stages of Nonprofit Organizations
Where You Are, Where You're Going, and What to Expect When You Get There
by Judith Sharken Simon with J. Terence Donovan

Shows you what's "normal" for each development stage which helps you plan for transitions, stay on track, and avoid unnecessary struggles. This guide also includes The Wilder Nonprofit Life Stage Assessment to plot and understand your organization's progress in seven arenas of organization development.

128 pages, softcover   Item # 069229

The Manager's Guide to Program Evaluation:
Planning, Contracting, and Managing for Useful Results
by Paul W. Mattessich, PhD

Explains how to plan and manage an evaluation that will help identify your organization's successes, share information with key audiences, and improve services.

96 pages, softcover   Item # 069385

The Nonprofit Mergers Workbook
The Leader's Guide to Considering, Negotiating, and Executing a Merger
by David La Piana

A merger can be a daunting and complex process. Save time, money, and untold frustration with this highly practical guide that makes the process manageable and controllable. Includes case studies, decision trees, twenty-two worksheets, checklists, tips, and complete step-by-step guidance from seeking partners to writing the merger agreement, and more.

240 pages, softcover   Item # 069210

The Nonprofit Mergers Workbook Part II
Unifying the Organization after a Merger
by La Piana Associates

Once the merger agreement is signed, the question becomes: How do we make this merger work? *Part II* helps you create a comprehensive plan to achieve *integration*—bringing together people, programs, processes, and systems from two (or more) organizations into a single, unified whole.

248 pages, includes CD-ROM   Item # 069415

Nonprofit Stewardship
A Better Way to Lead Your Mission-Based Organization
by Peter C. Brinckerhoff

You may lead a not-for-profit organization, but it's not your organization. It belongs to the community it serves. You are the steward—the manager of resources that belong to someone else. The stewardship model of leadership can help your organization improve its mission capability by forcing you to keep your organization's mission foremost. It helps you make decisions that are best for the people your organization serves. In other words, stewardship helps you do more good for more people.

272 pages, softcover   Item # 069423

Resolving Conflict in Nonprofit Organizations
The Leader's Guide to Finding Constructive Solutions
by Marion Peters Angelica

Helps you identify conflict, decide whether to intervene, uncover and deal with the true issues, and design and conduct a conflict resolution process. Includes exercises to learn and practice conflict resolution skills, guidance on handling unique conflicts such as harassment and discrimination, and when (and where) to seek outside help with litigation, arbitration, and mediation.

192 pages, softcover   Item # 069164

Strategic Planning Workbook for Nonprofit Organizations, Revised and Updated
by Bryan Barry

Chart a wise course for your nonprofit's future. This time-tested workbook gives you practical step-by-step guidance, real-life examples, one nonprofit's complete strategic plan, and easy-to-use worksheets.

144 pages, softcover   Item # 069075

Community Building

Community Building: What Makes It Work
by Wilder Research Center

Reveals twenty-eight keys to help you build community more effectively. Includes detailed descriptions of each factor, case examples of how they play out, and practical questions to assess your work.

112 pages, softcover   Item # 069121

Community Economic Development Handbook
by Mihailo Temali

A concrete, practical handbook to turning any neighborhood around. It explains how to start a community economic development organization, and then lays out the steps of four proven and powerful strategies for revitalizing inner-city neighborhoods.

288 pages, softcover   Item # 069369

For current prices or to order visit us online at www.FieldstoneAlliance.org

The Wilder Nonprofit Field Guide to
Conducting Community Forums
by Carol Lukas and Linda Hoskins

Provides step-by-step instruction to plan and carry out exciting, successful community forums that will educate the public, build consensus, focus action, or influence policy.

128 pages, softcover   Item # 069318

Collaboration

Collaboration Handbook
Creating, Sustaining, and Enjoying the Journey
by Michael Winer and Karen Ray

Shows you how to get a collaboration going, set goals, determine everyone's roles, create an action plan, and evaluate the results. Includes a case study of one collaboration from start to finish, helpful tips on how to avoid pitfalls, and worksheets to keep everyone on track.

192 pages, softcover   Item # 069032

Collaboration: What Makes It Work, 2nd Ed.
by Paul Mattessich, PhD, Marta Murray-Close, BA, and Barbara Monsey, MPH

An in-depth review of current collaboration research. Major findings are summarized, critical conclusions are drawn, and twenty key factors influencing successful collaborations are identified. Includes The Wilder Collaboration Factors Inventory, which groups can use to assess their collaboration.

104 pages, softcover   Item # 069326

The Nimble Collaboration
Fine-Tuning Your Collaboration for Lasting Success
by Karen Ray

Shows you ways to make your existing collaboration more responsive, flexible, and productive. Provides three key strategies to help your collaboration respond quickly to changing environments and participants.

136 pages, softcover   Item # 069288

Lobbying & Advocacy

The Lobbying and Advocacy Handbook for Nonprofit Organizations
Shaping Public Policy at the State and Local Level
by Marcia Avner

The Lobbying and Advocacy Handbook is a planning guide and resource for nonprofit organizations that want to influence issues that matter to them. This book will help you decide whether to lobby and then put plans in place to make it work.

240 pages, softcover   Item # 069261

The Nonprofit Board Member's Guide to Lobbying and Advocacy
by Marcia Avner

Written specifically for board members, this guide helps organizations increase their impact on policy decisions. It reveals how board members can be involved in planning for and implementing successful lobbying efforts.

96 pages, softcover   Item # 069393

Board Tools

The Best of the Board Café
Hands-on Solutions for Nonprofit Boards
by Jan Masaoka, CompassPoint Nonprofit Services

Gathers the most requested articles from the e-newsletter, *Board Café*. You'll find a lively menu of ideas, information, opinions, news, and resources to help board members give and get the most out of their board service.

232 pages, softcover   Item # 069407

The Nonprofit Board Member's Guide to Lobbying and Advocacy
by Marcia Avner
96 pages, softcover   Item # 069393

Keeping the Peace
by Marion Angelica

Written especially for board members and chief executives, this book is a step-by-step guide to ensure that everyone is treated fairly adn a feasible solution is reached.

48 pages, softcover   Item # 860127

Funder's Guides

Community Visions, Community Solutions
Grantmaking for Comprehensive Impact
by Joseph A. Connor and Stephanie Kadel-Taras

Helps foundations, community funds, government agencies, and other grantmakers uncover a community's highest aspiration for itself, and support and sustain strategic efforts to get to workable solutions.

128 pages, softcover   Item # 06930X

A Funder's Guide to Evaluation: Leveraging Evaluation to Improve Nonprofit Effectiveness
Peter York

More and more funders and nonprofit leaders are shifting away from proving something to someone else, and toward *im*-proving what they do so they can achieve their mission and share how they succeeded with others. This book includes strategies and tools to help grantmakers support and use evaluation as a nonprofit organizational capacity-building tool.

160 pages, softcover   Item # 069482

For current prices, a catalog, or to order call ☎ 800-274-6024

Strengthening Nonprofit Performance
A Funder's Guide to Capacity Building
by Paul Connolly and Carol Lukas
This practical guide synthesizes the most recent capacity building practice and research into a collection of strategies, steps, and examples that you can use to get started on or improve funding to strengthen nonprofit organizations.

176 pages, softcover   Item # 069377

Violence Prevention & Intervention

The Little Book of Peace
Designed and illustrated by Kelly O. Finnerty
24 pages (minimum order 10 copies)   Item # 069083
Also available in **Spanish** and **Hmong** language editions.

Journey Beyond Abuse: A Step-by-Step Guide to Facilitating Women's Domestic Abuse Groups
by Kay-Laurel Fischer and Michael F. McGrane
208 pages, softcover   Item # 069148

Moving Beyond Abuse: Stories and Questions for Women Who Have Lived with Abuse
(Companion guided journal to *Journey Beyond Abuse*)
88 pages, softcover   Item # 069156

Foundations for Violence-Free Living:
A Step-by-Step Guide to Facilitating Men's Domestic Abuse Groups
by David J. Mathews, MA, LICSW
240 pages, softcover   Item # 069059

On the Level
(Participant's workbook to *Foundations for Violence-Free Living*)

160 pages, softcover   Item # 069067

What Works in Preventing Rural Violence
by Wilder Research Center
94 pages, softcover   Item # 069040

ORDERING INFORMATION

Order online, or by phone or fax

 Online: www.FieldstoneAlliance.org
E-mail: books@fieldstonealliance.org

 Call toll-free: 800-274-6024
Internationally: 651-556-4509

 Fax: 651-556-4517

Mail: Fieldstone Alliance
Publishing Center
60 Plato BLVD E, STE 150
St. Paul, MN 55107

Our NO-RISK guarantee

If you aren't completely satisfied with any book for any reason, simply send it back within 30 days for a full refund.

Pricing and discounts

For current prices and discounts, please visit our web site at www.FieldstoneAlliance.org or call toll free at 800-274-6024.

Quality assurance

We strive to make sure that all the books we publish are helpful and easy to use. Our major workbooks are tested and critiqued by experts before being published. Their comments help shape the final book and—we trust—make it more useful to you.

Visit us online

You'll find information about Fieldstone Alliance and more details on our books, such as table of contents, pricing, discounts, endorsements, and more, at www.FieldstoneAlliance.org.

Do you have a book idea?

Fieldstone Alliance seeks manuscripts and proposals for books in the fields of nonprofit management and community development. To get a copy of our author guidelines, please call us at 800-274-6024. You can also download them from our web site at www.FieldstoneAlliance.org.